Distant Shores

By traditional canoe from Asia to Madagascar

Sally Crook

Impact Books

First published in Great Britain 1990
by Impact Books, 112 Bolingbroke Grove, London SW11 1DA

ISBN: 0–245–60044–2

Typeset by Photoprint, Torquay, Devon

Printed and bound by The Guernsey Press, Guernsey

For my mother and father

Acknowledgements

I am most grateful to Bob Hobman for allowing me onto his expedition, and to my parents for not showing their worry and thereby making me feel guilty about taking part.

I would also like to thank those who helped and supported us in any way, including Peter Welch, Philippine Airlines, Nelly who looked after crew members in Manila, the staff of the Argos tracking station in Toulouse, the authorities and people of the Philippines, Indonesia, the Cocos (Keeling) Islands and Mayotte, the Captain and crew of the *Epée*, the French Foreign Legion in Mayotte, helpers in Bali and Father Franz Lackner on Savu and Rote.

My special thanks go to the other members of the crew for their tolerance and good humour, and to the staff of the Indonesian Embassy in Antananarivo as well as the Malagasy government and people who welcomed and entertained us.

Thanks are also given to Melissa Shales who helped me to edit the manuscript, and to Jean-Luc Barbanneau for publishing this account of the *Sarimanok* expedition.

Contents

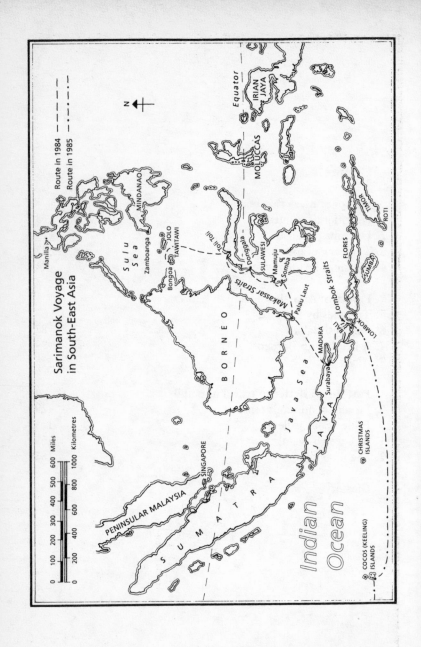

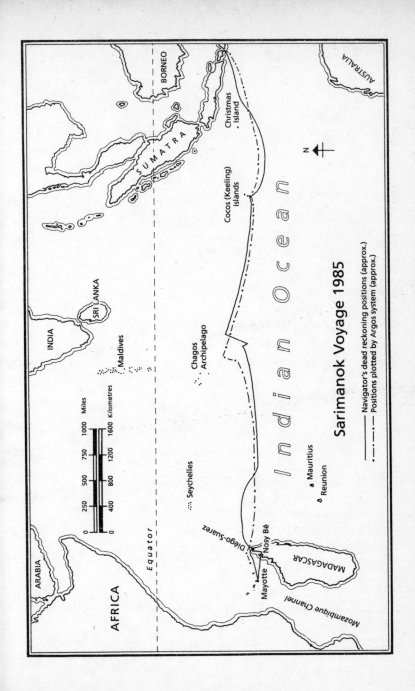

Sarimanok Voyage 1985

— Navigator's dead reckoning positions (approx.)
—·—·— Positions plotted by Argos system (approx.)

Part one
Bless this boat

1. Nutritionist wanted

As we crossed the small stretch of sea to the harbour steps, Chico began once more to froth and rave.

'Stop it!' Bob cried desperately, jumping off the rubber dinghy. Steve and I followed.

'Grab the other end of the stretcher! Hurry!' They waded off into the darkness, splashing their way as best they could through the thigh-high water.

I was left in the sea holding the dinghy's painter, wondering quite where to fasten it. Then, in the light from the shore, I saw the thick pilings that held a warehouse above the waterline.

'They'll do.'

I had to keep my head and be practical. Hindered by the weight of my skirt swirling around me, I waded into the gloom of the arcade formed between two rows of pillars and wrapped the rope around one. I surprised myself at the detached way in which I raised the outboard into the cocked position and checked to make sure a swell could not throw the motor against the concrete. Then, taking note of the dinghy's position, I too forced my heavy way through the water to the steps.

It seemed to be a holiday resort kind of town. I wrung some water out of my skirt as I walked along the pier, and had barely put my sandals back on when I spied a girl, a waitress perhaps.

'*Dimana orang barat sakit*? (Where is the sick Western man?)' I asked. She set off at such a pace that I had almost lost sight of her by the time the police station came into view. It was obvious from the throng of people pressing their faces to the windows that this was where our patient was laid. Inside Steve was cooling his fevered forehead with ice from the *es campur* vendor, while Bob conferred with the officers on duty.

'It's not the first time I've been in one of these,' Steve observed with a grin as we climbed into the back of the police van, and Bob seemed to forget the plight of his friend in a haze of reminiscence about previous encounters with the law. Every now and then the van jolted, our comatose patient groaned, and we were drawn painfully back to the present.

It was Saturday night and the technicians were off duty. Between explanations to the police about the irregularity of our visas, I looked back to where the doctors were taking a blood sample in the hospital corridor and was horrified later to see an enormous spinal puncture needle projecting from Chico's back like an arrow. Cats wandered at will through the wards, and relations of inmates slept in the corridor. What chance was there here that he'd survive when they didn't even know what was wrong?

Mosquitoes attacked my ankles below my soaking skirt while I waited at the basement kiosk to buy medicines, drips and urine bag. Had I come to Asia for this? To become attached to people just in time to see them die? Expeditions are meant to be dangerous and exciting, but somehow I had expected it to be like the films, where everything came right in the end. This wasn't right, and was it the end? On that miserable Saturday night in Java I thought it might be and did not bargain for the adventures still in store for us.

'Miss Crook? I'm Bob Hobman,' the expedition leader greeted me as I descended the aeroplane steps to join him under the shelter of his enormous Philippine Airlines umbrella. I had flown in stages from rainy Gatwick to even rainier Bongao, the main town of the small island of Tawi Tawi at the south-western extremity of the Philippines. Standing in the midst of the downpour, while Bob read the letter I had brought him from a friend in Manila, I had time to study the man who was responsible for my being here.

He was tall, thin and very suntanned, his face crumpled and aged more than his physique, which was clothed in loose casual shirt and light-coloured trousers. He had a posh English accent, in spite of years spent in 'Austrayliah'. It seemed incongruous with his rugged features and lifestyle, but was delivered in a powerful, chesty voice more compatible with his outdoor appearance. His speech was all the more surprising because his letters had brought to my mind's eye a 'laid back' American, still chasing his dreams after all his Sixties' contemporaries had sunk into regulation urban materialism and obesity.

Bob was apparently in tune with Asian customs and waited more patiently than I for the baggage to be delivered and for the driver from Philippine Airlines to collect us. Before moving off, two of them sat down, drank a beer and smoked, discussing the rebel and pirate situation in the area as the sky cleared.

'We'd better go wide of the coast in front of the estuary mouth.'

'Yes, it's easy for boats to hide behind the small islands there.'

A double-outrigger canoe with outboard motor, which the 'Cadastral Boys' (the surveyors for the proposed road to 'our' village,) had put at our disposal for the day, was waiting behind a dingy wooden warehouse. We stowed my bags, the rough guitar I had bought in Zamboanga and the bottle of duty-free champagne I had been instructed to bring for the launching, before motoring north-eastwards.

I was looking forward to reaching the house that Bob and his friend and expedition co-leader, Chico Hansen, had built, but the use of a boat and outboard motor was too rare an opportunity to waste and we stopped off at a small offshore island on the way to do some background filming for the documentary that was to be made of the journey.

Some of the wooden houses were built over the sea, supported on stilts, with the white sand and coconut palms embellishing a postcard scene which did not quite belie the poverty there.

'*Salamat siang! Apa kabar?* (Good afternoon! How are things?)' Bob sang out by way of general greeting before a foot had been placed on the wooden pier. He spoke easily with the people in *Bahasa Indonesia*, which many of the men had learnt by working (illegally) in Borneo. This was nearer than mainland Mindanao and populated by fellow Muslims with whom they probably felt a closer affinity than with the majority of Filippinos, who are Christian. I spoke a little Malay/Indonesian which I'd learnt on a journey in Indonesia a few years before – Malay, altered slightly over years of usage, is the lingua franca of Indonesia – but I was out of my depth here; my perception of any but the most superficial aspects of these people's lives was necessarily coloured by Bob's interpretation of them.

Our visit seemed to generate a holiday atmosphere and we were followed by troops of children and not a few adults, who very rarely saw foreigners. We watched the agile men climbing high coconut palms and inspected possible building materials for the *Sarimanok*. We were seen off at the end of our visit by a large number of the villagers, who pointed skywards with expressions of cheerful resignation to the heavy clouds that darkened the day, soon to empty themselves upon us again.

I had become involved with the expedition after applying for the post of nutritionist on a '7th-CENTURY RAFT FROM THE PHILIPPINES TO MADAGASCAR' which I had seen advertised in a pencil-written note on a noticeboard in the college where I was working. I duly applied in writing to the Liverpool address quoted, and then began to worry that I would actually be chosen, especially once it became clear that I was the only applicant. That was about all the information I could get, while friends wore gloomy expressions and prophesized disaster.

'Telex the Philippines to be briefed for the sailing expedition as soon as possible,' my mother telephoned one late December evening. 'And buy a red ensign fifty centimetres long,' she added irrelevantly. I had indeed been 'chosen' from the staggering number of applicants.

Of course there was no question of refusing the opportunity. My telexed acceptance to someone at PAL (whatever that was) asked a lot of silly questions such as 'Do I need a life jacket?' and 'What kind of insurance should I get?' – when a succinct 'What the hell have I let myself in for?' would have been infinitely more to the point.

I had long been interested in Madagascar's unusual heritage, peopled by immigrants from South-East Asia as well as nearby East Africa. Further reading revealed that most people believe the migrations from the east took place sometime after 500 BC, the date I later discovered the expedition was in fact to be based on – not the seventh century as quoted in the advertisement. Sometime during the first five hundred years of the Christian era was the most quoted period, and the migrants were generally agreed to have flea-hopped around the coasts of Asia and Africa, settling in Africa before crossing to Madagascar, rather than to have sailed straight across the Indian Ocean as we planned to do.

The coastal route is safer and therefore a more logical choice, especially to people who did not know what lay far to the west of them. There is also some evidence of Far Eastern influence along the mainland coasts. But these are not the only reasons for championing this route – some writers put forward the theory that the vessels of the period would have been incapable of sailing directly across the wide Indian Ocean. It was the challenge of doing it the hard way, and stifling this particular quibble, which seemed to have prompted the expedition.

I found out from libraries in London and two letters from Bob, that it was not rafts, but double-outrigger canoes (which sit low in the water and, with their decks extended on to the outrigger supports, resemble rafts) in which the migrants would have made their voyages. Unfortunately I could find little about the food of the period, but in the short time I had before leaving, I tried to devise a traditional diet for the crossing, deducing what plants and animals would have been available by a process of elimination of those known to have been introduced by later migrations to island South-East Asia.

The exasperating lack of information from PAL (Philippine Airlines), which told me only to 'bring sleeping bag, net and all required until Bali', sent me into a state of catatonic anxiety, but by now I was hooked, and if I had been dismissed from the project I would have been eaten up by disappointment and thwarted curiosity. I was worried about casting in my lot with people whose abstention from illegal or nefarious activities could not be guaranteed, but Bob and Chico were also taking a risk. As Bob so aptly put it in his letter: 'It is slightly irregular to prepare to spend seven months on a boat with someone I haven't clapped eyes on but I'm willing (on behalf of the rest of the crew) to take the risk if you are.'

So I took the PAL ticket and the plunge and, with barely enough money to get back home in an emergency, reported for duty in the Philippines.

During the boat journey up to the village where the *Sarimanok* (named after a legendary Philippine bird) was being built, I tried to extricate some basic facts about the expedition from Bob, but without a solid base upon which to build pertinent questions, it was like asking a foreigner for bread without the necessary vocabulary and being given only jam. He had lived with his dream for so long that he could not separate the groundwork from the embellishments and, like a man voicing only the occasional snippet from his train of thoughts, could not conceive of the listener's inability to piece together the whole story.

I did become engrossed, however, in the real-life stories of terrorist activities here in the southern islands of Mindanao, which were the titbits of information offered today. Many of the Muslim people of the southern Philippines resent administration from Christian Manila and some of the more discontented 'Moros' are waging a guerilla war against the Government who, from the American-orientated perspective, revile them as 'Communist rebels'.

As with all breakaway movements, there is also some dissension among the rebels, so even this Muslim stronghold can be dangerous for residents and visitors who could get caught in the crossfire. The presence of modern pirates, whose activities have become more widespread in the area since the sea exodus of ethnic Chinese from Vietnam, makes the area especially dangerous for people travelling by sea. As a result, foreigners cannot usually visit this trailing archipelago at the south-western tip of the country, and Bob and Chico had gone to great pains to get permission, because of the abundance of all kinds of wood for boat building. The village they inhabited, Languyan, was headed by a former Moro rebel, who, after more than ten years living rough in the forest, had been bought off by the Government and made Vice-Governor of the area. He had imported his Muslim Tausug friends and relations to live among the Samal further south, and it was from these imported people that Bob had been recruiting his boat builders.

They had been disappointingly slow, however, and at the risk of offending the Vice-Governor, Bob had found some Christian Chavacano craftsmen in Zamboanga. They were arriving that day, along with Chico and two other crew members, on the 404 ('four-o-four'), a passenger boat which served this string of islands.

Our house was built of wood and bamboo, on stilts though not over the sea, and had a nipa palm roof. Its position on a hill meant that one entered at the door at ground level but surveyed the village beside the sea from balcony height. I was privileged as the only female to have a 'room' to myself. This extension had just been completed (no tedious applications for planning permission needed here) and the chest-high partition from the main room afforded privacy only if others chose to observe it – in other words, not to observe over it.

There were no doors, other than the one to the outside, and the main room, where Bob and Chico slept, was continuous with the kitchen, which overhung the lowest part of the hill. All rubbish, bio-degradable or not, was thrown through the unshuttered window, since no qualms about environmental pollution had yet been aroused to trouble local consciences. At the end of the passage between the main room and 'mine' was the 'shower', a small area at ground level, where an oil drum full of water could be ladled cold over the bather's head to trickle down to the feet, robbing the body of its heat, before dripping away through the floorboards.

A green cockatoo, generally referred to as 'The Parrot', sat in indignant captivity on a twig suspended from the eaves by the open-sided passage to the shower. His restive body was secured there by a disc of coconut shell which was threaded through a large hole on to the branch, a smaller eccentric one circling the resentful bird's leg. To reach the shower one ran the gauntlet of this malevolent creature from the right and a face full of silk from the left where a spider spent part of each night spinning, only to have its web destroyed every morning by the first person to blunder into it in their drowsy stupor.

The whereabouts of the outside loo was betrayed by the well-worn path leading down to it. Housed in a small wooden hut, it was a neatly-made 'long drop', with a wooden board surrounding the hole to prevent slipping in the mud left by the frequent rain. Accurate marksmanship was hindered by the ants that scampered over my feet as I squatted. They obviously relished the pee splashes on the wooden board, and the agitation caused by their unwelcome attentions ensured further supplies. I rated the facilities quite comfortable but could see I would not be having a leisurely Sunday morning read there.

Ants swarmed in their millions in the house, too, because of the sap and fruit in the trees which constituted some of the corner posts. They marched in single file along strings holding up mosquito nets and washing, in columns down beams and in platoons over bed posts. The only place they seemed disinclined to explore was down the strings to The Parrot's perch.

When the 404 arrived half an hour after our disembarkation, I did not run out with the villagers to witness its progress up the channel to the wooden quay since I did not yet realise what an infrequent sight this was. Soon after it docked two new crew members, Greg Condron and Steve Corrigan, crested the hill on which our house, the 'Teahouse of the Mango Moon', was perched, away from the more modest village houses. They burst enthusiastically on to the scene together with Chico, a handsome man, slightly shorter than me but exuding an aura of physical power.

Against my better judgement, I was immediately attracted to Chico. In spite of my decision that amorous adventures with members of the crew would be disruptive and unwise, I had already been charmed by his photo in a publicity article Bob had sent. His long greying hair, then drawn back in a ponytail, had now been cut to a length more conventional for his unbelievable fifty-four years, but the small French-style beard he still sported enhanced his Latin mien. The impact was purely physical, of course, and I looked forward to the release from suppressed lust that the revelation of his true character would surely bring.

While little boys carried supplies from the mainland up to the house, the three spoke animatedly of their hair-raising journey. The boat had been overloaded and had begun to fill with water in choppy seas. The bilge pump had broken down and the frantic crew had thrown much of the cargo of cement and some of the passengers' possessions overboard to save the ship. Chico, Steve and Greg, trying to sleep on the roof of the cabin, had to brace themselves on the guttering board and, with each exaggerated roll of the vessel, found themselves swinging wildly from horizontal to vertical. These ferries quite often sink on their two- or three-day journeys. One had capsized only the previous week in the shark-infested Sulu Sea, ensuring that there were no survivors among the hundred or so passengers. Owing to a rather old-fashioned chivalry, I had been singled out for a safe flight to the island but now felt cheated of an experience so exciting in retrospect.

'Bring out the *Milikan tubig!*'

This apparent reference to something oversized and Irish translates as 'American water', or alcohol. Añejo rum is cheap and plentiful in the Philippines, and, since it is the sailor's traditional drink, was happily adopted as our regular tipple. The fresh supply had luckily been spared the sacrifice to the deep for the safety of the ship. As night fell, a bottle was opened, cigarettes were expertly rolled, and the evening was spent listening to further tales of the two-day voyage. Greg, still indignant at the memory, gave a self-conscious imitation of the homosexuals who had pestered and bated him on the journey.

'They wanted me to go below deck with them. They made eyes at me. Aaah!'

While in Zamboanga, they had bought some chickens, even hauling over a sackful of special food from the mainland, but on arrival we found that a couple of cockerels had been slyly substituted for two of the females. One of these had only one leg and the other had not survived the journey. After their traumatic sea crossing, moreover, the chickens did not lay for several weeks and the few eggs eventually obtained must have cost at least US$15 each!

José Florentino, a highly resourceful and inventive man from Manila, who spoke English, Tagalog (the main Philippine language), Tausug, Samal, Chavacano, Chinese and Japanese – at least – squandered his talents out of material necessity and helped about the house, occasionally giving technical advice. His wife Fabiana, who spoke the Chavacano language, which is very much like Spanish and therefore became a means of communication between us, was doing the cooking. The whole business of being in the kitchen was entertaining as long as I was not its only occupant. As a nutritionist, I had dreaded the inevitable erroneous assumption that I was also a good cook and so was pleased to see the post was already filled. My relief was short-lived, however, as I found I would have to cook here on land to practise for the voyage.

I do not hate cooking itself and even acquiesced in a letter to being the 'nutritionist-sailor-cook' when I found that was the exact designation of the person required on the boat. It is the daily housewifely drudgery of cooking for others which is oppressive, with the fear that the long-awaited meal will turn out badly, an eventuality which can easily be borne when cooking only for oneself. With the added difficulty of learning to start and tend a wood fire as the only means of cooking here and on board, I hoped somehow to delegate the job frequently.

Another task also awaited me, and this was even more nerve-wracking. Villagers had greeted me as 'Doctor' when I first stepped from the canoe, and when I had opened my mouth to dispute the title, Bob admitted to having broadcast this misinformation to secure for me a respect which these Islamic people would not normally accord to a lone woman on a boat full of men, where she could only be regarded as the 'in-flight entertainment'. Since M.Sc.s in nutrition and entomology would mean nothing to them, in the time it takes to put out your tongue and say 'Aaah!', I had donned the guise of MD and was that very night called out to my first patient.

Soon after the pressure lamps were lit, I was shown reluctantly down to the village to see a boy with colic. Bob accompanied me along the dark path that ran behind the stilt-borne houses. The whole family lived in one room and the prostrate boy was moaning gently on his mat bed on the floor, surrounded by relations of all ages. His abdominal pain was more intense on the lower right side and I feared appendicitis. The 404 was back from the mainland but would probably not leave again for weeks. There were no roads linking the villages on the island and, even if the people had had transport to the airport twenty-eight miles down the coast, they could not have afforded a flight to the hospital in Zamboanga.

Luckily, Bob, who had some previous experience in Indonesia as a doctor, came to my rescue. Finding no recoil pain, he gave the lad pills to reduce the spasms, skilfully nursing me through my first attempt at diagnosis. I was launched upon my bogus medical career with no more ability than many of the local people, though they still consulted me, partly because of a groundless faith in the superior ability of Westerners, but also as a way of tapping our store of otherwise unobtainable medicines.

People took to forsaking the medical post, which was perfectly adequate as long as you had malaria or were pregnant, and the nurse left the village, never to be seen again. I was exasperated by the unwelcome responsibility which had been thrust upon me, but also felt a terrible burden of guilt when the medical post collapsed, perhaps permanently, because of my short stay.

2. Dubious paradise

Monday, 6th February

Went out quite late in search of the boat. The others, who had already been to inspect it, came back boisterously declaring that it was 'looking good', though I did detect a note of forced gaiety in their voices. I stayed on the path, thinking a boat that must be at least the size of a Royal Navy lifeboat would be visible between the houses, but found nothing. In the afternoon Chico led me to the construction site. I was horrified – no wonder I had missed it! The *Sarimanok* is no more than a hollowed out tree-trunk, about forty-five feet long, which the boat builders are still honing down with sharp *patoks*. Seven or eight people could hardly sit side by side in this, let alone live, cook, eat and sleep on board for two or three months!

Chico explained how the heap of enormous planks on the shore will be used to build the sides up. She will grow considerably, but it's obvious that it will be some time before we sail. The few days I had been led to expect we would spend in the Philippines stretch ahead into weeks.

Tuesday, 7th February

The southern Philippines are beautiful, a blissful conjunction of coral reefs, blue sea and sky – all that a 'rich', healthy foreigner like me should want. I am here to work, but with few books in which to research the ancient diet, and with the apparent lack of food here to collect and dry for the voyage, I do not have any pressing duties specific to my role as nutritionist. So time passed easily today, the house crowded with people to consult the 'doctor', to socialise, to stare or simply to pass the time until the rain stopped.

This morning, Greg, Bob and I went out for a dive over the reef across the creek, the water glassy smooth and glinting in the sunlight. I looked down on white sand, washed into ripples by the tide, and an expanse of clean coral strewn with pom-pom-soft sea-anemones, as I allowed myself to be paddled in the *banka* to the best area of the reef. One of the men dived to anchor the boat by the painter to a rock on the bottom, while I reflected that macho male pride can have its compensations.

I'd never dived before but soon found out how to block the snorkel mouthpiece with my tongue to prevent my mouth filling with water during a dive. Blowing the head of water from the tube on surfacing, we took on the appearance of a school of small whales, and as the others swam further and further to sea, their periodic spouting was the surest indication of their whereabouts.

When the anchor rope unloosed itself from the rock, I was the only one aboard. I paddled frantically away from the shore where the boat was being driven by the tide, but seemed to be losing the battle and was worried that I'd smash José's *banka* on the reef in the shallows. The others were too far away to hear me shouting and it seemed an age before Greg returned, triumphant, with a large cuttlefish that he had speared, to get things under control again.

Thursday, 9th February

We acquired a couple of bodyguards on our walk in the wood today – men carrying armalite rifles to protect us 'from the wild pigs', but who might just as easily have had rebels in their sights. After visiting the shacks the men live in with their wives and children, pale and wan-looking from the rigorous poverty of their lives, and giving away some left-over breakfast snacks, we set out on a path crossed and recrossed by wide tracks made by the pigs, each strewn with the debris of their forced passage through the undergrowth. The excuse for the excursion was the need for fruit, but, finding no citrus as we had hoped, we rested and drank the sweet water of immature coconuts hacked open by a *bollo*, allowing the soft flesh, scooped from the shell by wedges chipped from the fibrous nut covering, to slip down our throats like jelly.

Greg has already voiced some doubts about the expedition and talked to me conspiratorially of how dissatisfied he is with the little information he has managed to glean so far.

'They're not being straight with us,' he complained.

'Yes, there's something secretive about them. Where are they getting their money from, anyway?' I added my doubts to his.

'Peter seems to be financing a lot of it,' he replied. (I don't even know who Peter is.)

Although he can't put his finger on what particularly rankles, he feels cheated and deceived, as if there's something important we need to know but are not being told.

True, we were not in on the inception of the project, but we are being treated like children who should not worry their heads about details, and indeed, have no right to ask questions. If this were a large, well-planned operation, I would feel confident to leave the leaders to make arrangements while I busied myself with a small corner of it, but large and well-planned are the last adjectives I would choose to define this expedition. It seems to be the result of a brilliant idea (Bob's), which two men (Bob and Chico) have had the courage to carry out, but the flaw is the need for a crew which is bound to cause complications.

Though I would never have considered following through such an idea myself, I had grasped the chance to take part in this expedition, able to do so only because we were not expected to pay our own expenses. I did not know then where the bulk of the money was coming from, though our constant need to dip into our pockets, with a promise of future reimbursement, told us that we were struggling.

Greg tried at every opportunity to winkle Bob from his protective shell but each prod sent him deeper in, parrying the attacks with denials that there was anything more to know. Greg's agitated state of mind was compounded by his overpowering wish to get to sea. He had recently got married and only countenanced the separation from his wife for three or four months because it should have been a time filled with excitement, a last adventure before settling down. His heart must have sunk even lower than mine at the sight of the scarcely-started boat, and he was enraged that Bob had not told him the true state of things before he had agreed to come.

After several days his questions became more direct.

'When will the boat be finished so we can leave?'

'How should I know? I'm only the organiser. It's already taken longer than expected,' Bob replied patiently. Unappeased by the reasonable tone, Greg persisted:

'You must know more than you claim to. Why aren't you both being open with us?'

'There is nothing to explain,' Bob replied, puzzled. 'I can't make The Boys go any faster.'

The arguments continued while I, too cowardly to support Greg, pretended to read in the corner but listened avidly to all that was going on.

'I'm sorry about this. It must be upsetting,' Chico soothed me when he tired of the battle. 'Greg doesn't seem to be fitting in as well as you,' he added, mistaking my silence for contentment, though he sometimes said he thought I was full of 'questions I wasn't asking'.

Bob and Chico were fighting a hard battle. They too were impatient to be off, having already lived on the island for seven or eight months, and before that being trapped by weeks of negotiation in Manila. The pace of life in Asia is such that, even by nagging and wheedling the authorities, foresters and carpenters unceasingly from the moment of their arrival on Tawi Tawi, all that Bob and Chico managed to achieve was to get their chosen trees felled, dragged miles to the sea, and the rough shape of the hull dug out. To retain outside support and goodwill, Bob, when writing each monthly report of the expedition's progress for the sponsors, had to disguise some plans as recent accomplishments, so everyone not in sight of actual progress was deceived.

Information about everything, from the rebel past of the Vice-Governor to the source of the funding for the expedition, seemed to be on ration, and was delivered in frustratingly small instalments over days or weeks as the subject came up for discussion again and again. Finally, however, the funding fable emerged thus. One trip to Zamboanga on mainland Mindanao had brought Bob and Chico into contact with Peter Welch, a film producer from Australia completing a documentary on the pirates thereabouts. Intrigued that they were living on an island usually forbidden to foreigners, he asked if they ever saw pirates.

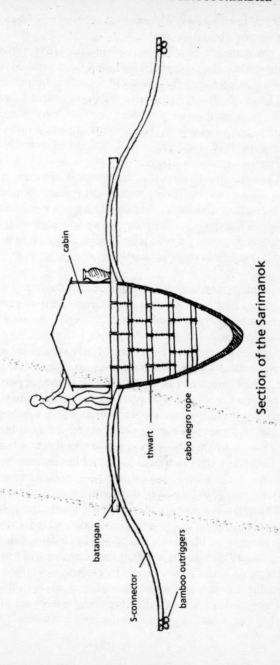

Section of the Sarimanok

cabin

thwart

cabo negro rope

batangan

S-connector

bamboo outriggers

'They're all pirates! We see them every day!' (An exaggeration but certainly based on fact).

Peter's interest had then turned on their business there and, impressed by the venture, he had found independent sources of funding to help the expedition and provided equipment for Bob and Chico to film it. Along with the ticket concessions granted by PAL, their troubles seemed to be over; but the money supply was erratic, partly because of the difficulty of getting it to them, and they were still living hand-to-mouth, saddled with the upkeep of daily wages to their workers.

The many frustrations they faced would have defeated most people long ago, but their patience and renewed optimism after each crushing disappointment or setback was miraculous. Each strengthened the other, helping him up when his spirits were down and, luckily, nether stayed long enough in the pit of despondency for their sojourns there to overlap.

The construction site was a magnet to the children. I wondered whether a board screen would discourage them or whether it would actually draw people to peer through the knot as on urban building sites.

Sarimanok's hull had been honed finely enough by now. The gunwale planks were to be mounted next, bent to the shape of the dugout hull, and tied down. The outrigger support beams or *batangans* would then be placed across them. The bamboo outriggers would rest on the water each side of the boat, their springy S-connectors allowing the boat to sit low or high in the water, and, by their buoyancy, preventing the boat from rolling. *Sari* would be wide as well as long, and her present construction site among the village huts could no longer accommodate her. She had, therefore, to be moved to an area beyond the village.

The hull was already in the water, the wood parings being carried away with each outgoing tide. It was now righted and pushed out into the creek with men inside to paddle, trailing behind them the long planks that would build up the gunwales. An uncertain cheer went up on launching, followed by a silence, as of people holding their breath, which subsided only when it was seen that she did not sink. A launch towed the developing boat closer to the mouth of the inlet, where she was drawn ashore again beside a coconut palm grove and a single stilted house. Next day a scaffold would go up and building would really begin. It started to rain as the hull came ashore: a good omen according to Chico. Obviously the locals didn't agree and they raced for shelter, believing that rain on the head causes headaches.

Although we had arrived only six days before, Greg decided he could not wait for the boat to be completed and would return to Australia. He was to leave very early the next morning. As I passed him to go to bed, he shook my hand and said he was glad to have known me. The pain at losing his dream of adventure after weeks of anticipation was obvious from the intensity of his gaze and the tautness of his body. Predictably, whenever the others talked later of his accepting defeat, they would imply it was due to cowardice.

Work on the *Ajung* ('big boat' as the locals called the growing *Sarimanok*) continued in fits and starts. The new workers from Zamboanga were industrious and worked quite well with the Muslims. Bob would invite them to the house from time to time, where he would reiterate their qualities like a praise-singer, as they alternately hung their heads as if in shame and smiled shyly at the compliments. They spoke English quite well and would sometimes stay throughout the evening, as our dinner got cold in the pot and Fabiana chafed to be away. Their wages of about US$1 per day were very high and therefore a great incentive. These frequent doses of flattery also probably did much to bolster their egos and enhance the work, and were probably no less an encroachment on their free time than they were an annoyance to the rest of us.

The Chavacano boat builders ('The Boys') were staying in the L-shaped pork-packing factory that was in construction at the foot of our hill, beside the sea. 'V.G.', or 'Vice', as the Vice-Governor was so aptly referred to, had struck upon a plan to make the village prosper – hence the pork-packing factory – a plan which would not only attract the entire shark population of the Sulu Sea to these shores, damaging the fishing, but also could not fail to disgust and offend the Muslims of the village, especially the Alhaji who lived close to the premises.

Antonio Quijano, the leading shipwright, was skilled in his profession. He loped about the site, pencil pushed through the crown of the straw hat he had appropriated from Bob. Large and ponderous, he did not tight-rope walk along the thwarts and gunwales with the agility of Willy, José (another one) or Ricardo. The same age as Bob (forty-four), but with a family to support, he and the others on the boat lived frugally and guarded jealously their accumulating wages, although these cannot have been very secure, hidden somewhere within the open-sided pork-packing factory.

José, the boat builder, was a quiet grey-haired man to whom I hardly ever spoke. Willy was small and wiry, with long hair, and looked like a Rolling Stone. His thin face creased down the cheeks when he smiled at his nickname 'Willy the Peg', earned by his skill in making and inserting these wooden alternatives to nails.

Ricardo seemed older, though his nickname was Boy. His specs gave him a bookish responsible appearance, and his frequent excuse for the delay in finishing the boat was that, since a woman was to board her, they had to make sure it was safe. I found myself wishing that the men in these poor countries would show the same concern for their own women, who were constantly risking their lives in too-frequent childbearing and overwork. Ricardo was talkative and friendly and, when I expressed a preference for his company among The Boys, in their absence, I was mocked with loud guffaws and cries of 'Oooh! Sally's got the hots for Ricardo!'

Almost every day there would be some hitch in boat construction. There was no more *cabo negro* (black hairy bark from which rope was twisted) to sew the planks together; one of the local workers had been appropriated by V.G. to work on the 202 launch; or the whole village was celebrating a funeral which involved day-long feasts at the expense of the unfortunate bereaved family for a week. Bob and Chico rose each morning with renewed optimism and determination, only to be told of the latest setback. Refusing to allow themselves to be beaten, they would always come up with a solution, but each hiccup took its toll.

V.G. was a source of many difficulties since he could not decide whether to be pleased that the expedition was focussing benevolent eyes on his island, or whether he should try to milk the 'rich' foreigners on his patch for all he could get. The tree which formed the hull of the *Sarimanok* had been felled with great effort by hand, narrowly missing killing a man, on Bob's birthday, and was understood to have been a present to him from Vice. When the bill for goods and services was presented towards the end of our stay, however, the tree was itemised there at a cost nearing US$1000. (I doubt if it was paid for.)

The absence of clear-cut duties made me feel guilty, and I was loath to spend my time as if on holiday for fear of being thought lazy or apathetic. Realising that a nutritionist on a boat is the most dispensible of the crew, I wanted to remain in good graces so that I would not be left behind when the real adventure began. Walking down to the building site each day, I found that though I did not possess the strength to carry out the actual labour of boat-building adequately, I did have the power to reason out solutions to structural problems. My own plans voiced on the site were usually ignored, however, while Steve's, which often amounted to the same advice more technically expressed, were greeted with 'Good thinking, Steve!' and promptly acted upon.

So, finding myself unwanted for the 'men's work', I kept fairly busy at home with housewifely activities, even though Bob apparently suspected me of sleeping all day. He had made a risky stand for 'women's lib' simply by allowing me on the expedition, but his lack of respect for my views on almost anything except my nutrition speciality (and even this he often disputed) usually robbed me of a fair hearing.

My air of reproachfulness must have been galling, however. When Bob taught us some knots and how to splice ropes one evening he obviously resented my ability to pick up the complicated procedures almost immediately.

'You've got it wrong,' he said and proceeded to explain the knot again in an avuncular manner. I hadn't, but when I put the rope down on the table, proudly implying that I needed something a bit more exacting to keep me amused, the warm glow of 'being right' quickly changed to a hot flush of shame as I realised how childishly annoying I was being.

I was envious of the men's freedom to walk around from dawn to dusk in only a pair of shorts, since casual dress on women is deeply frowned upon in many countries, and virtually a crime in Muslim areas. I wore only shorts and T-shirt inside the house, but wrapped a piece of cloth as a sarong around my waist whenever I went out. I sometimes forgot, however, and, when we reached Indonesia, where I wasn't known, had to cover up again. It was only then that I realised the full impact of my behaviour and felt ashamed of the discourtesy I had shown to the people of Languyan.

Against José's advice, I also took to walking barefoot as Bob and Chico had been doing for months without encountering any chiggers – fleas or mites that bore into the feet from the ground and swell with eggs. It gave a wonderful sense of freedom from which stubbed toes were a poor deterrent. I enjoyed the opportunity to walk over and see the state of the *Ajung* most mornings, so, grasping a few fresh fish by the grass stem threaded through their mouths and out between their gills, I walked down the hill and along the coastal path to the coconut grove to deliver them to The Boys.

Children were always at play outside the houses along the route and would shout out, '*As-salaam alaikum!*', to which I replied, predictably, '*Wa alaikum as-salaam!*'

The greeting and reply could be repeated four or five times while one was still in earshot, and the children usually were. Our moods could be gauged by how long we would continue with the game.

Steve was to be the navigator on the trip and, since the methods used were to be traditional, like everything else on the boat, he needed to learn the constellations. He had brought a sort of 'Noddy's guide to the stars' from Australia, but it had been produced in Britain and was mostly concerned with the northern skies. We all spent time out on the grass of the hill beside the house or on the roofless balcony beyond my room, staring upwards, searching for those stars visible at the time. These included the Southern Cross, Gemini and, the only one I already knew, Orion.

Moonless nights were best since the sky was a darker backdrop on which the stars and planets shone steadily or twinkled, some with a red or green tint. Celestial bodies over cities are so often hidden from the eye by street-lamp glow, even when the night is clear of clouds. I had often looked up and appreciated the free display of bijouterie, but I had never before tried to intellectualise the experience. Far from exploding the magical beauty of the sight, the exercise increased it.

The choice of Steve as navigator was one of necessity. A well-known Hawaiian navigator, an acquaintance of Chico, who also came from Hawaii, had been asked to come, but it was apparent that he did not relish the challenge of sailing in an untried boat of traditional materials as well as design, even though the navigation would not have tested his abilities at all harshly. Steve's wide experience of sailing did not encompass practical navigation, thanks to the snobbish attitude of established perpetrators of the art who do not allow others to gain the skill and topple them from power. The responsibility of it was a worry to him, and he was often studying his books and observing the stars, waiting up to all sorts of unsociable hours to see every pattern that the night sky at that latitude could show him. He joked about his abilities, and his customary groan on getting a bit drunk was, 'I don't know where I am!' – more than a little disconcerting to the rest of us. We nicknamed him on these occasions after a famous namesake, Wrong-Way-Corrigan, who, in 1938, flew from New York to Dublin. This would have been a fair achievement except that he had set out for Los Angeles and had misread the compass.

The forest was a long way from our doorstep, and wood for boat building was heavy and cumbersome. Too many trees had already been felled to make the side planks for the boat, since length and suitability could not always be gauged until the timber was inspected in its recumbent state. We agonised over the wisdom of using the forest like this, though we did appreciate that the cutting of relatively few trees in an otherwise little-exploited forest was better than overfelling for the production of furniture or laying waste whole tracts of land for agriculture which would be exhausted in a couple of years.

The effort of hauling the tree for the hull had been enormous, so further wood supplies were sought near the water, further along the coast. *Ligayen*, an especially hard and heavy wood, was needed to be bent into the S-shaped supports for the outriggers. A supply had been found along the coast near Padang Pantai and all of us except Chico, who had had his fill of such expeditions, set sail up the coast on the 102 to collect some.

Thursday, 15th February
We sailed out for the wood today. The launch had a gun mounted on the foredeck – fortunately it remained unmanned and covered

by a cloth on the hour-long journey. I saw Vice for the first time coming in the other direction from mainland Mindanao. He seems scared of sailing but even more unwilling to fly to Bongao and risk being sniped at by former rebel 'colleagues', as he sails past their area of control on his way up the coast to Port Languyan.

The pier of Padang Pantai is a rotting, rickety construction of wooden slats on stilts. We felt like intrepid circus performers walking along the narrow planks, arms held out balletically for balance, until we noticed men and women of all ages almost skipping along the boards, without seeming even to look where they placed their feet.

We set off with guides and the boat builders on a gruelling stumble through the mangrove swamp to inspect the wood that has already been felled. The mud sucked the shoes off our feet at each step. Abandoning them, we squelched barefoot through the ooze, dragging each foot with great effort from the swampy ground with a slurping noise like that of a spoon scooping out jelly from a bowl and sinking to ankle depth in the sun-warmed mud. It would have been quite pleasant had it not been for the mangrove roots which spiked our soles.

We were fed back at the village. Then Ricardo arrived to report that the launch was going tonight and we would be left behind if we didn't hurry down to the quay. Having stumbled halfway along the pier to the boat, we discovered that San Miguel beer was on sale at a shop opening on to the pier, and after several weeks' necessary abstention, we sat down, delighted to drink and socialise with the Samal people. For some reason Steve found the last few yards of the boards much easier to negotiate afterwards!

The tide is out, so there is no danger of our leaving without the timber we have come for, but the boat is listing steeply and it will be a difficult night, trying not to roll on to the sleeping bodies of wiser passengers nestled against the lower gunwale. Meanwhile we seem to be providing the floorshow for the crowds on the pier.

As soon as we arrived on deck, we pounced on the bags that contain the long-sleeved and -legged garments for protection from insects. A nauseating reek emerged from Steve's.

'Oh no! My bottle of Añejo has broken,' he wailed and hastily reshut the bag to contain the smell. He has chosen to do without his soaked shirt and trousers, has acres of bare skin exposed to the ravages of mosquitoes, and is hiccuping from the shock to his digestion of having eaten a whole chilli pepper in bravado. I also hear a muttered complaint that he doesn't know where he is.

Friday, 16th February

Steve is covered in bites, and we have nothing to alleviate the itching, so, along with a hangover headache, he is having to soldier on. The little toe I wrenched on a mangrove root yesterday is so swollen that I can't draw on my shoes, but the warm mangrove mud was soothing.

Setting off to collect the wood, we commandeered a *banka* this time, our lazy progress upstream watched by small iridescent green or blue fiddler crabs which retreat only momentarily into their burrows before emerging to pick delicately but rapidly at the tiny particles of food in the mud. The males looked funny holding up their outsized orange claw, like a boxer's protective glove, in an effort to attract a mate.

The timber was lying in the wood close to some 'fox holes' built by rebels and probably used to store ammunition and food rather than to sleep in. Living rough in such a rainy, mosquito-ridden swamp must be excruciating and the sense of injustice which drives men to live such a life incredibly strong.

Bob filmed the men bringing the 'lumber' out from the wood. To cover the long distance to the sea, it was floated down the creeks, the depth of the water increasing from calf-high to thigh, chest and shoulder. As the bottom fell away and I found myself swimming, I hoped that there was no truth in the rumour that crocodiles had been seen in the area.

It was obvious that the boat builders had more fundamental worries. It was soon apparent that very few of them can swim, and as they waded deeper and deeper they resorted to scrambling as best they could from one exposed mangrove root on the vertical bank to another. The wood should have helped and I expected to see them holding one end of a log like learner swimmers with outsized water floats, but much of the wood was very heavy or waterlogged and sank in to the murky creek, where I'm sure some pieces must have been abandoned. I cannot conceive how they managed to get the wood out to the launch, anchored fifty yards out to sea. Even holding on to the *banka*, the distance seemed enormous through eyes only inches above the grey choppy sea, and I was relieved to reach the ship's side.

Chilly in my rubberised jacket and trousers as the only windproof garment to hand, I pitied the less well-equipped boat builders, shivering and exhausted on the journey homeward.

Chico's welcome home this evening was enthusiastic. He is pleased to have missed the ordeals of the trip but has been lonely and gave me a hug. I pretended not to care, but over the two weeks of our acquaintance I have been dismayed to find that he really is a 'nice guy'. It isn't going to be easy to keep my feelings to myself.

3. The gang of four

'Bloody rain!' Steve said in a pained, rising tone. His half-mocking complaint became his habitual cry as the weather made work outside difficult. It could be pleasant, however, to sit in the gloomy interior of the house on a rainy afternoon with the flames of a fire Bob had lit casting flickering shadows, the only bright spot of activity in the sombre room. Fireside dreams could be indulged more comfortably than in the gas and electric fires of a British winter.

'Yahoo! We've got some goodies!' Chico reported as he brought in a box from the boat which had ferried V.G. back to the island. It included a load of novels for Chico from friends in Zamboanga, and at the bottom of the box, some American dollars were stashed with the movie film.

'What a lot of hooch. Good old Peter!' Bob cried enthusiastically, forgetting his countless differences of opinion with him for the moment. 'Now I can pay the men, at last.'

The boat departed again soon, for Jolo, where V.G. had an appointment to kill or terrorise the men who had recently murdered his cousin. (At least, that is the form in which the story reached me.) The prosecuting of vendettas was quite normal here. It was like living with the Mafia in Sicily or with prohibition in America – all right as long as you do not get involved – and Zamboanga was, and still is, like a gangster-infested Thirties' Chicago or New York with daytime murders and street shoot-outs. The arsenal from which the weapons of hand-grenades and guns were loaded on to the boat (and two days later returned unused) was the nearest building to ours. We could do nothing about this but, whenever armed men came calling, Bob insisted they leave their armalites outside the door.

I rose late by local standards, at about 7am, but was unable to do anything useful until my stomach's demands had been met a couple of hours later. There were no foods such as fruit, bread or biscuits, which could be eaten raw or without further preparation, so I cooked breakfast myself on a couple of occasions and learnt early on that taking the initiative like this was tantamount to volunteering for the duty permanently.

Oatmeal porridge was a special favourite of Bob's and we all gratefully fell into the habit of eating it for brekky too, until the supply was exhausted and 'quacker oats', as José called them, gave way to dry white rice. This insipid dish was eaten in great quantity by the more prosperous of our neighbours, though we usually made it more palatable with sugar, or condensed milk when available.

My version of porridge rapidly became a brekky talking point. I was never quite sure how much water I should use and it was therefore never of the right consistency. When it was especially thick, Steve asserted the indispensability for the voyage of someone who could produce such good caulking material for emergency repairs to the boat. When it was thin, it prompted numerous Oliver Twist impressions as they all held out their bowls for more gruel. When a glance through the floor slats to the chickens' night quarters finally revealed an egg or two, I thankfully began to make pancakes as a variation.

I went to bed early (between 9.30 and 10.30 usually) because, in the poor light, it was difficult to read the few novels we circulated amongst ourselves. But I was often kept awake by the noise and light which could not be excluded from my room, even though the men tried to lower their voices. They often talked, smoked and drank, sometimes until 3 or 4am when they would retire, exhausted but relaxed and sometimes intoxicated, and begin snoring loudly within minutes. I would remain wakeful, not so much because of the noise but because of the rage seething inside me at the injustice of it all.

I usually woke before dawn with excitement, anxiety or the pins and needles caused by the board bed on my bony hips. I felt guilty sleeping in the afternoon when I was supposed by the others to have slept all night, so was always tired and must have behaved during the day like a manic depressive.

The disadvantage in retiring early was that I missed some interesting conversations, though listening from my bed I heard things I may not have been meant to hear. When discretion made them belatedly lower their voices even more, I was always tempted to call, 'Speak up! I can't hear you!'

Chico was often, in Bob's words, 'good value'. He mimicked his Spanish mother and Norwegian father's accents, and while eavesdropping from bed, I was sorry to miss the effusive visual effects which accompanied his tales of action. He continued his vivacious displays of Hawaiian and Tahitian dancing at parties long after we younger expeditioners had flaked out on the beds and benches around the living room, and his slapstick performances with the imaginary creepy crawlies on his bed were side-splittingly funny.

Chico was particularly prone to itchy mosquito bites, although he slept under a net which Bob had no need of. He blamed the irritation on bedbugs or fleas and one evening, reading glasses perched on the end of his nose, he went on a purge, examining the surface of his bed minutely, while grumbling like a cantankerous old man. He hit gleefully at each fleck of soot and sand, or picked a tiny flake of dead skin from himself and swore it had been biting him.

I am interested in entomology, but cockroaches and ants are not my favourites – though we seemed to be theirs. Ants found their way into everything.

'What can I do about the ants in my guitar?' Steve asked. 'It's not a problem I've had before.'

We didn't know, but hoped that strumming a brisk tune would cause a stampeding exodus from the sound hole to escape the earthquake.

Solitary wasps nested inside hollow wood or built their own houses of paper or mud. Spiders were abundant too, of course.

'Perhaps they'd like some of these flies,' Chico said gleefully one night, and he batted one with the palm of his hand into the web of one particularly ferocious spider in the roof beams. The awful arachnid approached quickly, making the web vibrate by a straightening and flexing of the legs like a trampolinist testing the springs. Perhaps this made it look larger and more frightening, though to a trapped fly it must have looked horrendous enough.

The spider then rushed at the fated fly, sank its fangs in and devoured it within a few seconds.

It was a good game, but the spider was soon full and subsequent gifts, though equally terrorised, were merely paralysed and co-cooned in silk.

'Look at that! It's wrapping it up for later.'

'Anyone for Take-Away?'

A cruel joke, but people usually kill insects slowly and painfully with insecticides. This method seemed positively humane by comparison.

'Hey, don't female praying mantises eat the males?' Steve asked.

'Sometimes.'

'Before or after mating?' he asked facetiously, as if sure of the answer.

'During,' I assured him.

(Gulp.)

Rats plundered the leftover food in the cooking pots and their numbers increased steadily in spite of poisoned bait being put up in the rafters. They clattered over the pots at night and their family life could be followed like radio soap opera from the noise of their fights and nest-making in the roof over our beds.

Chickens, ours and other people's, became bolder the longer we harboured the sack of special food, and would get inside the 'Teahouse' at every opportunity. They soon found they could fly in, and a morning or afternoon spent in the house would be punctuated every few minutes by the need to shoo them out by girating like a demented scarecrow. It was more tiring than a day's work on the *Ajung*. Some panicked when cornered and tried illogically to press their bodies between the bamboo slats of the kitchen wall; when one was wanted for the evening meal, however, it would fly straight and true to the nearest unshuttered window.

Dogs, too, were a problem at the house and whenever they came near we threw stones at them to try to set up an invisible boundary around us. A catapult was also pressed into service and some of the men became quite adept at placing a painful but harmless stone on the animals' buttocks, sending them away with a heart-rending yelp.

Our novelty value in the village palled after a week and the little boys no longer came to sing and play their ukelele to us in the evenings. We turned instead to our ant-riddled guitars or accompanied the small cassette-player in song, crooning the deliciously sentimental 'The Mountains of Morne' in mawkish unison with Don Maclean, or gruffly asserting that we were 'Sailing' with Rod Stewart.

And there was always star-gazing . . . and sometimes the need to make some adjustments to the position of the boat at high tide. One dark night, we trooped down in single file to retrieve the *pamalong* (stem or sternpiece) from the shallows where it had been soaking.

'Hi ho! Hi ho! It's off to work we go,' we chorused as we marched down the hill, only to return, having found the task completed by the conscientious boat builders, singing the appropriate homeward refrain. The sense of togetherness made me pleased to be 'one of the boys' (or dwarves, in this case) and not the solitary Snow White.

Steve was an easy-going man and a good friend. I enjoyed an equal measure of disinterested comradeship in return for my liking for him. Bob was difficult to get on with, but I appreciated his charms when I was not maddened by his criticisms. Above all, I admired his spirit of adventure. The four of us knew we should tread carefully because of the danger of an explosion between people always in each others' company, but after a month, our *ménage à quatre* had worn in quite comfortably, like an old shoe. I almost dreaded the anticipated arrival of two Americans, young friends of Chico's, as their absorption into the group would necessarily destroy it.

The fact that we had all become friends showed in our ability to insult each other without giving it a second thought. One evening, as we clustered around the lamp to read, Chico pointed to me and complained to the others, 'She called me a twit!' and, in a stage whisper to Steve, 'What's a twit?'

'Well, you're one,' he explained unhelpfully.

We assured him of the mildness of this British form of abuse but he did not seem convinced. Differences in American, Australian and British English were a constant source of amusement. Chico's pronunciation of buoy ('boo-ee') passed into *Sari*-talk, especially after the arrival of another American; and my surname, Crook, being Australian slang for 'ill', was too good to be true in a 'doctor'. Though we did not learn much of the local languages, we became trilingual amongst ourselves: in the morning we ate 'brekky' and fed the 'chooks', and when the need arose we could go to the 'loo', the 'john' or the 'dunny'.

On a couple of evenings we borrowed a radio from the school-teacher in the village, but after we learnt from the BBC World Service that the pattern of wars and political upheaval had not changed, we fell back into our state of blissful ignorance, unconcerned about soccer violence or floods in our own home areas which seemed so remote.

Amongst our pooled books there were a few good ones, though with the turmoil of my excited mind I could not concentrate on anything very deep. We would whet the appetite of those waiting in line to read the book we were engrossed in by broadcasting particularly amusing anecdotes of Tom Sharpe, or pithy phrases of John Mortimer.

Bombard's account of his incredible journey across the Atlantic in a lifeboat without any stores of food or water was our Bible, and Gavin Young's *Slow Boats to China* was read dutifully since he had journeyed through this Sulu Sea. His most perilous adventures were all in this area, and, reading his story, my worst fears for the journey were reawakened.

Some people in England had cited the pirates as the icing on the cake of this adventure, considering their activities to be the stuff of swashbuckling boys' comic stories. Bob, Chico and Steve, however, had some horrific tales, gleaned by Peter Welch while making his pirate documentary, and, since we had no means of protection, I was bewildered by the calm way in which Bob and Chico regarded the possibility of attack. Nothing short of giving up the journey would obviate the danger though, and I had to learn, like them, just to hope for the best.

Their attitude seemed to me to be very naïve – not only on the pirate question, but also in their faith in the robustness of the boat they were building and in the honesty and goodwill of the people helping. José spoke to me of how they would be cheated and how we would never finish the boat and get away, but he 'knew his place' and would not interfere. I kept wishing he would be more forceful though, since his opinion was more greatly valued than mine, and any complaints from me at their apparently easy-going attitude would only label me as a 'wingeing Pom'. When it was later revealed that some of the wood that had been offered for use in a strain-bearing part of the boat was considered too weak even to make orange boxes from, I became still more troubled by their inexperience.

Expertise has to be gained somehow, of course, but I had a niggling sense of their lack of responsibility and unfitness for the task they were undertaking, since they seemed to repeat their mistakes rather than learn from them. Far from being reassured as plans for the expedition became clear, I became ever more anxious.

My own attitude towards the people in the village remained somewhat timid. I could not speak the local languages, but communicated with Fabiana in Spanish, with one or two Indonesian words thrown in, which approximated to Chavacano. Most of the boat builders spoke English, as did Vice and his mother, so our gossip about the politics of the island had to be hushed and it sometimes deteriorated into mouthed words across the table, since her house was nearby and our conversation probably audible.

V.G.'s mother was a dynamic woman and I was intrigued by her skill in the homemaking arts. I enjoyed watching her and other women weaving large sleeping mats, and I had arranged to learn Filippino cookery from her, but the lessons never materialised owing to lack of ingredients.

Bob had imported most of our dry stores from the mainland since there was little here. Food in the village was dull and meagre. Local people could not afford to eat rice every day, but usually ate *panggi*, cassava partly cooked and dried and packed in plastic bags. It needed only to be toasted thoroughly in a dry pan until it browned a little and was quite enjoyable as a change from rice, but it is nutritionally poorer and therefore an inadequate staple food. I find rice tasteless and lacking in texture, so regarded the alimentary aspect of our stretch on the island and the boat with no bread and few potatoes with less than wholehearted enthusiasm. Bland, flaccid noodles, cooked to supplement the rice, weren't much better, even when disguised by tomato-paste sauce.

The fish was excellent, however, and preferable to the scrawny, tough chickens we ate on special occasions as a 'treat'. Succulent *lapu-lapu*, tuna and parrot fish were caught by the Badjau people and some were sold to the other inhabitants of the village. The Badjau are often referred to as 'Sea Gypsies' because of their nomadic life on the sea. Their equivalent of the Romany caravan was a cramped houseboat, on which they spent so much of their life that they never learnt to walk upright and in a straight line. It is not known from where the people originated, but they are now dispersed around the Sulu Sea where, wandering on the sea less frequently, they have abandoned the boat as a home. Now they live in wooden houses built on stilts over the sea into which, as in the past, they can spit or cast away their rubbish without rousing themselves from the hearth.

'Look at that!' Steve cried unnecessarily when the muffled sound of an explosion turned our heads in time to see a spout of water thrown up from the sea.

'They're dynamiting for fish,' Bob confirmed. 'It's illegal, but who's going to stop it here?'

'It's such a pity they have to destroy the coral to catch the fish,' I added, as we watched the Badjau, who lived in a community of stilted houses on the opposite side of the creek from us, jump overboard from their *bankas* and scoop up the stunned fish that floated to the surface before they could sink again. We knew they fished like this but had never seen it from the house balcony before. They must have been getting cocky, or desperate.

Without the Badjau there would have been little protein on the island, and when they were away on an extended fishing trip, there was no choice but to raid the henhouse for eggs or skinny birds. The Samal and Tausug here seemed only to venture out to sea for long enough to travel from one patch of safe dry land to another, and I was equally unenterprising in the art of fishing.

Few vegetables were cultivated, though José showed exceptional initiative in growing some on a small plot of land he had acquired. *Kangkong*, or 'marsh spinach', is a green-leafed plant that grows in swampy land, its spearhead-shaped leaves crouched among the grass blades and easily overlooked. Few local people, with the notable exception of the Vice-Governor's mother, appreciated the need for green stuff in the diet and, far from actually labouring to make the plants grow, did not even go in search of this nutritious weed. I launched a crusade, therefore, to persuade people of the efficacy of eating this vitamin-packed plant, but Chico's unselfconscious daily dose of enough vitamin pills to support a military platoon for a week had given this method of meeting the body's requirements the Western seal of approval, and my campaign was doomed to fail. I collected the plants for our own use, however, to improve meals and stave off the temptation to resort to pills myself.

Fresh fruit should have been plentiful in this wet tropical place, but even ripe bananas were a treat. Fruit began to grow but was never allowed to mature. Children would scramble for the small hard guavas that grew outside our open shutters and gobble them greedily. They must have been hungry, but I could not help regretting the lack of restraint that would have led to greater rewards. The food can have done little for their hunger pangs, though it may have masked them with colic.

An avocado tree graced the area in front of our house, and, as the avocado pear is not liked, we had plenty of them. Every couple of days during the season a few pears would be ready and we'd dole them out by the half or quarter, until, near the end of our stay, the simultaneous ripening of most of the fruit culminated in an orgy of guacamole.

Generous offerings from José's garden and occasional fruit from the mainland that was snapped up minutes after the boat docked also added to the limited variety of local produce. Condensed milk and tinned mackerel were sometimes available in the shops and were often the only foods for sale. I was very distressed to see the female proprietor of one of the shops feeding her baby with highly unsuitable diluted condensed milk. Tinned milk was beyond the buying capacity of most people, and even we thought twice before investing in a tin.

Despite the tedium of our diet, I could not stop myself from eating everything in sight, which did not go unnoticed, though the others were just as greedy. Perhaps it was the very insipidity of the food that encouraged overeating because, although hunger was satisfied, my craving for sweets could not be indulged here.

Luckily, I have always been thin. My time on the island increased my girth to record widths, but could do nothing to remedy the flatness of my chest. My hair had been cut very short before leaving home and the sun had tanned my face in uneven blotches. In short, I did not look very attractive and felt decidedly inferior when the others boasted of their girlfriends' good looks, comforting myself with the thought that relationships are not based on appearance.

One day, as Fabiana and I were grimacing with pleasure over lemon slices in soy and chilli sauce, José came in with an egg-plant and some beans from his garden, together with a few old twigs.

'This is *tubli* root,' he explained.

'Is it for us to eat?'

'Oh no. You better not do that. It paralyses fish. This will protect you: send sharks away.'

I could not see us rising each morning on the voyage and smoothing on *tubli* juice like Oil of Ulay on the off chance that we'd fall into the sea that day and need protection from sharks, but was touched at his concern for our safety, though not entirely convinced of the root's efficacy.

I realised soon afterwards that it was high time I got down to a bit of food preservation. Having acquired – oh wonder! – a whole stick of ripe bananas, I purloined a few for drying experiments. José and I cut them into slices of different thicknesses and laid them out on a table on the veranda in the sun.

The fruit and veg drying was not very successful, because of the humidity of the air and frequently overcast skies. Downpours began so suddenly that the slices of food would be quite sodden before they could be got under cover. The final result of several days' drying was sticky sweet banana slices that would have kept quite well in a dried milk or Milo tin – if we had not brought them out for a treat from time to time.

Clean water was piped from streams in the forest to a tiny pool at the bottom of the hill. Water collection was mechanised as soon as possible. I filled the large plastic jerry can with a bucket and fixed it with a mountaineer's clip to a thick, plastic rope stretching from the back balcony to the watering hole. Steve then hauled it up the hill by a thin rope which cut the hands to pieces, while I warded off the mosquitoes or just stood in the shade of a tree watching the humming birds hovering at the flowers above me.

The men sometimes bathed directly at the well, prudishly clad in shorts as local custom demanded, washing their private bits by hands thrust inside. Women showered at the wells too, but had to be even more covered from breast to knee by a sarong. I considered the hard slog of carrying water in jerry cans, when the rope was being used elsewhere, worth the effort for an effective shower.

'No work on the *Ajung* today,' Bob declared after a trip to the village. 'That man we gave the bouillon cubes and vitamin pills has died.'

'Oh dear, I hope they don't blame us,' I thought, rather self-ishly.

He had lived in the house next to the first building site of the *Sarimanok*. On my first trip down to watch the boat building I had been ushered up the short step-ladder and ducked my head under the low doorway to see this man of about fifty, as he lay on his hard bed. He had been a hopeless case, we had treated him with things that might not help but could do no harm. He was my first spectacular failure, but on the day of the interment we were invited in again to see the results of our handiwork, without a hint of reproach, and found the man laid out peacefully on his former bed of pain, with that waxy feel to his skin I had heard about in the dead. Few people sought my medical services in the next few weeks.

Peter Welch could not leave a cameraman permanently with us, so he had to hope for the best with Bob who had no former experience of the art of film making. Steve had taken on the role of sound man and struggled with a faulty Nagra to record during filming and to tape Bob's voice-overs back at the house.

Filming the Friday mosque was a joint project one lunchtime. The local men, usually clad in trousers or jeans, now wore sarongs, and the women covered their heads, but not their faces, and did not object to being filmed and photographed. The mosque was built partly over the sea like its neighbouring houses, and between it and the houses stood a wooden post in the water. To this were tied for periods of about twenty-four hours at a time people who had broken the law and were to be punished. Woe betide anyone so short that the high tide came up to his nostrils, though a short sharp shock like this was probably preferable to six months in prison. On the one occasion when someone was punished in this way during my stay, the post was unoccupied when I passed the site as a *banka* had brought the wretched victim back to land for a lunch break!

In spite of feeling useless, I sometimes went to the *Ajung* site to do small jobs, such as chipping out the nodes of split bamboo poles so that they could be placed around other uncut ones to strengthen them for use as booms. The skill of The Boys and the other boat makers was enjoyable to watch.

Ropes were made by twisting together strands of *cabo negro* creeper, after which three strands of this would be twined to produce thicker ropes. This was done by threading the three strands through three separate holes aligned in a piece of wood. The rope maker then turned the portion of rope already twisted and drew it gently towards him as the completed rope grew in length. This rope was very strong, but the small pieces of black fibre pricked into the hands when it was being worked and broke off there, leaving flecks of black just under the skin. This made the hands very sore and I was pleased that my ineptitude kept me from most of this.

Then bamboo had to be skinned – a thin layer of its outer covering being stripped off with a sharp *bollo*. This is done to lighten the bamboo and prevent it from splitting when it dries and shrinks, and it required some dexterity. It was curiously satisfying to watch the long, thin slivers ride up over the knife as it advanced smoothly towards its wielder, the thinnest curling into tight ringlets and lying on the ground like discarded Christmas gift ribbons.

The fashioning of a peg was also an art: chipping away at a small chunk of wood until it was cylindrical, though slightly wider at one end than the other. After the peg had been knocked into the hole drilled for it on the boat, a small wedge would be hammered with a mallet into a split made in each embedded peg to widen the outer end still further and hold it in place in the boat. The peg and wedge were then sawed off flush with the surface. The use of the unwieldy machetes and *patoks* for such delicate work as peg making was a necessity as there were no other tools available that could be so well sharpened and had enough weight to be effective, but the boat builders used them with great precision. Steve, Bob and Chico struggled somewhat to perfect the art.

A coarse but effective pair of large wooden callipers was used to measure the thickness of the hull at various depths until it was thin enough to take the planks. This required new, untried techniques and Bob and Chico spent fretful nights before the big day, the culmination of months of planning and worrying. The planks too had be whittled down to a suitable thickness and were to be joined to the hull by rope ties between the thwarts – cylindrical poles of wood fixed horizontally across the beam of the boat between special retaining brackets of wood on the hull and planks – and by 'stitching' with thin ropes. Bow and stern ends of the planks had to be bent by brute force and fixed to the sprits by pegs – another worry for the men.

While these traditional boat-building techniques were being rediscovered, they brought elation or despair to those responsible; though I, ignorant of even modern shipwright methods, could not enjoy their enthusiasm to the full, nor join in their erudite discussions of the best line to walk between using tried and tested methods and being true to the traditions they were trying to honour. I did, however, discover the real beauty of these man-made objects. The curve of a bow was obviously functional as it allowed the boat to cut through the water without wasted power, the waters parting symmetrically in a white spume to each side, but it gave the boat grace even on land where the efficiency of function was not yet an issue. The curve of the S-shaped beams which allowed for a little bounce in the outriggers was also beautiful beyond the efficiency of their function, and the neatly woven ties of rattan which held beams and planks tightly together were like faultless basket-work.

Picnics at Sunday lunchtime became routine, that afternoon being free time for The Boys.

'Bob, I think you should let the guys alone for one afternoon a week,' Chico had said, expressing my own thoughts, though Bob was convinced his enthusiasm for the growing boat would be shared by all involved and that they would want to live, sleep and breathe her all the time as he did.

While he chatted with The Boys, Chico and I watched the mud skippers looking like space monsters with their eyes bulging above the water to see the land they were about to set fin on.

'My brother should be in on this trip. He'd love it,' Chico told me. His brother was something of a hero to him, but he seemed none the less secretly relieved that he had not been able to join them on this journey. This was Chico's chance to prove himself to himself.

'I used to be an architect and painted and drew in my spare time, but I saw what development was doing to Hawaii and wanted out.'

He went to live in Paris, then in Cadaquez, Spain, to pursue his art full-time and had been heartened by the approval of Salvador Dali on his one timid visit to his house there.

Chico's thirst for adventure had made him rash, or daring, enough not merely to join Bob's chancy expedition, but to put in his own savings. He had never really been able to settle down and was obviously still searching like a teenager to 'find himself'. His philosophy gave him confidence, however. He believed we can do anything we dare to venture, and that God and the universe is contained within us.

He worked so hard on the boat that he rarely had time to draw or paint. Bob frequently told him to take a day off, but he was too conscientious and so anxious to get going on the voyage that he worked himself almost to the point of collapse. Perhaps he too was overconcerned about pulling his weight, though he pulled enough for two.

These picnic Sundays were the only chance he had to draw and, after our saunter in the shallows, he settled to sketch the *Sarimanok*. Needless to say, his activity was particularly intriguing to the village people, whose attentions soon drove him away from the group in search of solitude.

Occasionally Bob prepared a special meal. He stood by the fire, peeling vegetables, or directing others to do so, and adding fistfuls of spices, tasting with a self-critical expression of concentration on his face, then adding more. These meals were often late because, a night owl, he would not jump up to cook until past the hour when my stomach was complaining of neglect. The meals could be gourmet delights, or they could be disasters – Bob's extroversion and apparent creed of 'immoderation in all things' resulted in Italian tomato sauces that were too tomatoey, or Chinese food stiff with ginger root, which kept the digestion in a state of shock for hours.

One afternoon, I waited until everyone was otherwise occupied before attempting to make bread without unsolicited advice, but Bob, rising from a short nap, saw what I was doing and was unable to resist criticising my efforts.

His bullying was incessant but probably unconscious. You do not find many self-effacing, pessimistic jelly-fish taking on such daring projects as his, and certainly he was strong physically and sure of his rights. He could not have understood the deepening hole in self-esteem that the constant drip of his acid criticism could make in less self-assured minds. I was easy prey to his withering appraisal because I was only too aware of many of my faults, and any protests I made were tempered with caution to prevent my dismissal from the expedition, which may have been interpreted as weakness or admissions of guilt.

Bob was forgetful though. This could be annoying, but was sometimes benign and calculated, and manifested itself as his most endearing characteristic of not holding a grudge. Only minutes after an argument he would greet me cordially and even enthusiastically. When I went down to the *Ajung* to hand out pieces of the bread I had made, he greeted me cheerfully and showed me the new developments on the boat as he tried the doughy cake.

'Not bad for a first go,' he conceded. Chico was even more encouraging, feeling that it was virtually edible.

The addition of a nipa-palm roof to the back balcony converted it into a 'navigatorium', where Steve could spread out his tools and study the stars. Its completion was an excuse for a party, an activity of which our adopted village was glaringly short. The not-very-fatted chicken was ingeniously captured and swiftly dispatched by José, expertly cooked by Fabiana and eaten in a trice by whoever was fastest off the mark. With the weight of bodies bowing the floorboards during the dancing that followed, the chickens cooped in the netting pen below must have wondered if it was Christmas or Armageddon as crumbs of food and stray pieces of cutlery fell down through the boards.

During the festivities, Bob and I were called out to attend a man with stomach pains. Having ministered to him by the

gloom of a Nestlé tin lamp and promised to return next day, we
walked further along the quay to look at the moonlit Taiwanese
junk that had sailed in that morning. It was curved up at bow
and stem, like the oversized shoe of a tramp, the gunwale slung
between in a downward sweeping arc. We were invited on board
and scrunched our tall bodies through low hatches to goggle at the
tiny bunks the sailors slept on: even their short legs would have
to bend almost heel to buttocks to be accommodated. The vessel,
so beautiful outside, caused a nightmarish panic of claustrophobia
below deck.

'Open, please!'
'We need doctor!'
At 7am the next morning, I had already been up for a while and
had made the porridge when the call came. Throwing a cloth over
the completely naked and still comatose Bob, I opened the door.
It was Efking, a friend of Fabiana's, who hurriedly ushered in a
man carrying the eldest of her children, a girl of about ten. She
had a large gash on the knee, caused, it seemed, by a sea shell on
to which she had been pushed by a bully boy as they were at play.
The wound was gaping and would obviously need stitching, so I
was relieved to see Bob had been roused by the noise and was soon
inspecting the damage.

He was still not quite sober and was so slow and deliberate in his
movements that I felt like shaking him to hurry. His Asian attitude
was much better than mine, though, as it was more calming to the
girl. We had suture needles and thread, but no anaesthetic or ice to
dull the pain.

The table, littered as usual with books, torches, batteries and
lamps, was swept clear in a moment and the child laid upon the
newly designated operating table. Her frightened eyes rolled at her
two tormentors. Bob's 'hair of the dog' – a leftover glass of souring
wine – was perched on one corner as he chose a suitable needle.
Chico, having returned to his bed a couple of feet away after
giving the day a try and then thinking better of it, got up again
when the commotion rose to a level which could not be ignored.
He joined the non-aseptic operating theatre and 'surgeons', with
hands washed in Dettol, and gently held down the girl's legs,

encouraging her with compliments on her bravery, which she could not understand, but were nevertheless soothing.

Doctor Bob, being the more experienced surgeon, cleaned the wound and pushed the needle through the skin at one edge of the deep cut. It was tough, and the girl's crying rose to a wail as he exerted pressure on the point against the resistance of two fingers supporting the skin. The flesh on the other side of the wound was similarly lanced and the two edges were drawn together, with three neat knots tied between the ends of the silk. I cut the threads while Bob sipped his wine with a serene expression on his face, as if at a sedate garden party.

Four more sutures were needed. Between my suppressed frenetic activity and Bob's staid, steady work, the job was completed and the child, hurting at the knee but glowing at the testaments to her stoicism, was dispatched home at the head of a small procession of adults.

'What time is it? Is brekky ready yet?' Steve quizzed us as he emerged from his bed in the navigatorium, refreshed by sleep as from an exhilarating game of squash.

He had not heard the crying or screaming only yards away, and as he settled down to the now cold and coagulated porridge he returned to the sport of designing new functions for it.

'This would make good glue to hold the . . . Hey, what's wrong with you lot? Have I got BO or something? Why don't you sit at the table to eat your porridge?'

4. Blessings be upon you

'How's the girl? What's her name *today*?' Steve enquired as I climbed up the hill with the toilet bag which held the dressings and the Tuppaware medicine chest.

The patient's name was elusive, but I finally managed to remember Sahaya's name for several days running.

I went frequently to dress the leg and see how it was healing. Mostly it was not. The painfully inflicted stitches broke one by one as the flesh below swelled, curling the skin back so the wound looked like a pair of negroid lips. I began to believe my too-frequent attentions were delaying healing rather than hastening it, and this was borne out when, after two or three weeks of my ministrations, Sahaya went with Efking to her grandmother's home island, limping, and returned two weeks later skipping and playing, with the knee scarred but neatly closed up. I was happy to see the crisis was over, but my reputation as a healer took another nose-dive.

My house calls were an exciting event for the other children, who set up a chant of "lo Salee!' as the vibration of the board-walk pier out into the creek proclaimed the heavy step of a foreigner. When I rose to leave, they accompanied me to the edge of their territory with a new cry, then rushed back to canter along the private board-walk joining the backs of the houses as I walked along the path in front, congregating in the space between each house to chant 'Bye Salee!' until I had passed. Their cries continued until I was out of sight and brought a bubbly feeling of suppressed giggles to my stomach and a lift to my heart.

The proximity of these gentle brown people was soothing as smooth silk on warm skin. Being surprised in the supposed privacy of my room one afternoon by two adolescent girls who walked in, unaware that in *Milikan* homes permission is usually sought to do so, my annoyance was soon allayed by the caressing quality of their soft spoken words and liquid brown eyes.

The palpable sensuality of their presence was calming to me, but I pitied the boys their enforced celibacy with such delicious temptations as these around, especially as the girls' coquettish behaviour was given free play in the knowledge that their fathers' Islamic censure made them inviolate.

The local attitude to women made them, predictably, an inferior appendage to father or husband, although the attitude was much freer than in Arab countries. As is so often the case, the women seemed to work harder than the men – nor was their work light, including water and firewood collection even when they were pregnant. No doubt if there had been any cultivation here the women would have done that too. I considered myself lucky that I had not been born into this beautiful and oppressive place.

I was considered to be different, however. While helping to carry long poles of bamboo down to the *Ajung* building site, I was stared at and lauded as a strong woman, but I felt uneasily that, rather than striking a blow for women's liberation, I had put another nail in its coffin by showing a capability for even more tasks than those they were already expected to perform.

Mature women were often still beautiful. At home Efking sat wrapped in a sarong knotted above the breasts, long black hair flowing down her back. With her high cheek-bones and coffee-coloured skin she was a Gauguin model of Polynesian grace and beauty. She had four or five children and was used to hardship, but when she brought Sahaya to the house with the cut knee, her capable exterior was banished by a furrowed brow and sobbing voice as she fussed around her daughter, not calming down until a man had taken charge of the situation. I suspect, however, she was acting to draw attention and get quicker results. When she was later (unfairly, I thought) derided as a 'wimp' in our household, Bob said warmly, 'Mmm, yes, she's very feminine.'

Chico and Steve did not appear to find demeaning displays of dependence and lack of fortitude to be manifestations of femininity, but I felt choked with indignation.

The Taiwanese had been invited to lunch with us the day after we had eaten a lovely meal on their junk – definitely not 'junk food'. José astonished us all by showing he really could speak Mandarin, which was just as well, since our conversation with them would have been sparse otherwise. In the following days, we sponged off them as the locals did from us, exchanging the use of diving gear for fishing (illegally, we think) in return for their lovely garlic and onion.

The Taiwanese, although Asian too, were more of a novelty here than we were and we even off-loaded some of the attention we received on to them. When the Muslims brought in a wild pig they had killed in the forest – religion forbade them to eat it, though these lads did not mind killing and making a profit from it – we found it too expensive and dispatched them to the Taiwanese who were to us what the rich *Milikans* were to the Filipinos. The hunters did not return and we presumed they had found a market with the Chinese.

'Isn't it about time those septic tanks were arriving?' Steve enquired one evening.

'That sounds civilised. We're not staying much longer – it's not worth making those kind of improvements,' Chico replied.

'No! Septic tanks – you know – Yanks!'

'Oh!' Chico said with relief. 'Yeah, I guess they're on their way now.'

Next evening, the appearance of a boat we had not seen before at the little-used jetty at the bottom of our hill roused Chico and I to investigate. The boat was already leaving again as we approached, but had left behind a few Western-style bags and a tall, slim silhouette which caused Chico to speed up.

'It's Don!' he cried in delight, and the two hugged a greeting and gathered his bags for the trek back up the hill as a vague introduction was made to me.

Don King was the son of Chico's best friend in Hawaii. He and a fellow surfing enthusiast, Jim, had been invited to join the expedition, but Jim had other adventures crowding his horizons and Don had come alone. I felt a trifle jealous of Chico's obvious pleasure in his presence and a little prejudiced against his Americanness (though this was broken down substantially when he offered around the chocolate he had brought).

Don was tall, fair-haired and tanned, with toes splayed wide, as is the way with those who rarely wear shoes. He was only about twenty-two but had travelled widely, firstly in search of the perfect wave and, incidentally, to pursue his surfing photography. Then, when he had perceived, unlike most of his single-minded mates, that the countries he was visiting held enticements other than coastlines thrashed by mighty breakers, he had branched out into the wider world of photography. The surf still drew him, though, and his prize photo of a board rider, taken inside the tube of a roller, was truly spectacular. In spite of a late first night, he was up early next morning and many mornings after to roam the area for good shots while the sun's rays were horizontal.

Don had to breach the comparative privacy of 'my' room, where he slept on the floor with the end of his long legs under my fragile bed. I took care not to fidget too much for fear of crashing down on his shins, though he, true to his unruffled exterior, did not lose a wink of sleep over it.

Don's extreme self-confidence for his age tended to put people's backs up, but I suspected a touch of jealousy in Bob, and a little anti-US sentiment. We agreed, however, that Don, as a Hawaiian, was, like Chico, less materialistic and nationally arrogant than many Americans. He soon got the measure of the others' characters and it was a relief to complain to him of Bob's often unreasonable criticism, to which he was also subject.

'He seems to forget that he's mad with you very quick, though,' he said, only a few days after his arrival. But like me, he noted that Bob's claim of reverence for initiative in others was not borne out by his reaction to it, and came to curb his natural inventiveness. We soon had a mutual understanding which, by the time we reached Bali, expressed itself in the whispered phrase, 'Whatever you do, don't take the initiative.'

Since the death, my supply of patients was returning from a slow drip to an unceasing trickle and we had plenty of ailments of our own now. Steve had managed to drive the corner of a plank of wood into one foot, and, after seeming to heal, this began to swell with pus from a deep infection. He could not walk for days, and the infection was not truly eradicated for several weeks.

I had an infected cut on each foot which caused so much swelling that I could not bend my ankles. Chico temporarily replaced my usual nickname of 'My Gal Sal' with 'Orphan Annie' because of my ugly swollen legs. Both Steve and I soaked our feet in hot water with salt or antiseptic, but eventually resorted to antibiotics which

Bob seemed to use and 'prescribe' with gay abandon. The wrong sort was chosen and it did not work for either of us.

The mosquito bites on Chico's legs had become infected too.

'Is the clinic in session?' he asked almost apologetically, sitting down wearily on the bench after returning unusually early from work.

'I had to put these on,' he continued, pointing to the soft twigs twisted about his ankles, 'to keep the damn flies off of my wounds.'

'I've got swollen glands at the top of my legs now,' he added, though he didn't offer to let me confirm this!

Working on the boat one day, Bob missed the wood he was chopping at with his *patok* and embedded the tool in his leg above the knee cap. I heard the tale from Steve, who was more animated about it than Bob.

'Lots of yellow stuff spurted out!' he said. 'It was awful.'

'Oh God! That sounds like the synovial fluid. It must have been deep,' I said with awe.

'That sounds impressive. Is it serious?'

'That's what cushions the ends of the two bones and stops the cartilages from grinding together.'

'Yugh! It sounds horrible when you put it like that. It'll soon be alright though,' Bob assured us, and after the initial shock he did not make a fuss about his knee, even when it began to stiffen up.

He was stoical about the injury, but I was concerned at the draining of his knee, especially as he had no opportunity to go to a real doctor before we sailed.

Launching day was getting near and Bob was frantic, in his externally calm sort of way, to get the boat ready. He was also concerned to make the day of the launching a good one, since the Australian ambassador to the Philippines and the press would be there. He decided we should have Badjau music. He already had a *gabang*, a wooden xylophone, and I was dispatched with Fabiana in the *banka* one morning to cross the creek to find someone who could play it well.

Fabiana and I paddled the boat across, tied up, and climbed up onto a wooden walkway. On one 'patio' there were shark fins lying around and fish flesh out to dry in the sun. The fins would make good money if they could be sold to the Chinese on the mainland.

I entered one hut and discovered that the glint of the sea through the slats of the flattened-bamboo floor lit the scene from below, making the windowless house less gloomy than expected. A fire burnt precariously in a ceramic fire-pot on the three curved-over lips of which a pot was placed. Although the meal was hours away, the pot was already bubbling as the excited women and children gathered around, skirting the fire with practised disregard, occasionally pushing the protruding pieces of wood further under the pot.

Fabiana told them what was needed, but they said no one there could play the *gabang*.

'Vamos a una isla màs lejos, Sallee!' Fabiana suggested after consulting them.

'*Hay un hombre quien sabe tocàrlo,*' she told me.

We travelled to the beautiful palm-fringed island half an hour away by pump boat and were given a generous lunch while we waited for the *gabang* player to return from his fishing. He strode in, and though he was shorter than me, under his own low roof his air of authority gave the impression of great height. He had the light brown hair with a faint fair streak, common to many Badjau, that has further mystified anthropologists about the tribe's origins.

The last few evenings before launching were filled with unpicking sacks for caulking material. The jute was pushed into the cracks between planks in the ship's sides and later plastered with *boletik*, a natural resin, and coconut oil. The *katig* (outrigger) bamboos would not be ready for the launching and the S-shaped supports were not yet finished. The boat would have to be cobbled together for the show and we hoped the guests would not be expecting to see us sail away since it was clear the *Sarimanok* would not be seaworthy on the day.

Suddenly the eve of the launching was here and Chico had not yet returned from his trip to collect sail-cloth and rope. Peter Welch managed to get to the village with two cameramen from Australia, and a Filipino clapperboard man. It was good to see a few outsiders, and as I climbed up the hill with Peter he asked me how things were.

'Great!' I replied, because now that it seemed we would be leaving soon, they really were.

When the 102 sailed up to the jetty, I rushed down to see if Chico was back. Filipinos were disembarking, dressed in their city clothes of 'blue jeans', but carrying their shoes to prevent them from getting damaged as they picked their way along the landing stage of boulders. They were laden with boxes full of goodies from the mainland.

I climbed on board and found Chico up to his waist in the hold, passing things up to José.

'Hello! How did it go?' I cried above the bustle and noise.

'Oh! Hi, Sal!' Chico replied, absent-mindedly.

'You look brown. Been out a lot?' he added belatedly, as if sensing my disappointment that his pleasure at seeing me did not match mine.

'Are the film people here yet? Is the boat ready for launching?'

'Yes and no,' I replied, answering each question in order.

'But I saw them in Zambo,' he said, bewildered, being sure the boat must be finished by now.

'I mean yes the crew is here, and no the boat isn't ready,' I corrected him.

'Good! But, we can't back out of the launching now,' he said.

He began to unload our supplies carrying such heavy loads that I worried he would injure himself. Even Bob remonstrated with him about it.

'Don't be stupid, Chico. If you put your back out or something, the expedition will be ruined,' but he continued until most of the supplies had been carried home.

It was too late now to make the boat look presentable for the launching and we all settled down to an evening of merriment with the exuberant Aussies.

Monday, 26th March
Launching Day! We missed the dawn, emerging an hour or two later with the problem of the unseaworthy boat still unsolved.
I was impressed by the matter-of-fact way that Bob and Chico, driven by desperation, commandeered bits of rope and timber, and in a couple of hours tacked together a ship which roughly resembled their idea of the finished product.

When the call came that we should bring down tea and coffee, I was scarcely aware that the journalists had landed. I was hot and sweaty from bringing the rest of the supplies up from the launch, but there was no time to change out of my dirty everyday shorts and I was disconcerted, when I reached the shore in the guise of tea lady, to be transformed immediately into a celebrity.

The launching was meant to be at about three but the journalists were in a hurry. They flew into Zamboanga yesterday evening and sailed down to us overnight, but they couldn't spare more than a couple of hours on the island before getting back to 'civilisation'. We hurried to the meal that was provided for us outside V.G.'s house, the journalists still asking questions. The village people must be startled by so many foreigners here after years without a single visit from an outsider. The crowd passed the village three times, entertaining those who have never visited a city or seen the brisk way these strangely dressed people go about.

The meal over, we were hurried, with indigestion-guaranteeing swiftness, back to the *Ajung*. I rushed up to the Teahouse to collect the bottle of champagne, but, too elated now to worry about our scruffiness, did not seize the opportunity to change, remaining in my beach wear in solidarity with the others, who were still shirtless and unshaven.

I was given the honour of launching the boat and copied the standard incantation used by royalty.

'I name this ship the *Sarimanok*,' I said proudly, standing astride the bow with a foot on each gunwale of the still deckless boat, tapped the bottle on the stem *pamalong* . . . and dropped it unbroken in the sand below.

The bottle was passed up to me again and I smashed it hard against the boat this time, covering myself with froth. I got down quickly and the boat was dragged down into the shallows by a hundred men pulling on two ropes. V.G. was on board by now and he directed the operation with loud commands and heroic gestures, like a general sending his soldiers into battle. The men hauled the boat, chanting rhythmically to synchronise their efforts.

I looked at Bob, who appeared anxious that the hurried cosmetic work might collapse, or that she would keel over. When she successfully floated, he had tears in his eyes.

With the real business of the day over, the journalists scrambled to reboard the launch that took them back to the navy vessel anchored offshore and the cameramen and sound men were nearly left behind.

The mood of elation continued into the night. Fabiana was instructed to cook for a hundred people since we expected them all to stay for the party. Where to sleep them all is no longer a worry. The Badjau are still here, and one journalist has stayed on for the celebrations, along with an Italian photographer, but that is all.

Whilst wading out in the sea to capture the hauling in of the boat on film, the photographer tripped and wet cameras and lenses. He then went off in search of a hair-dryer and an electrified home in the village, and the party began.

The Badjau fisherman, procured at such cost in effort and money, disdained the *gabang* which he was brought to play in favour of the guitar which all of us can play. A man I have treated for an infected gunshot wound sang a 'duel song' in Samal, with a young woman, which was translated for us in snatches. It sounded hard and raucous, and was improvised as it moved along, each protagonist singing a verse in turn and trying to outwit the other in repartee.

Instead of the party ending as usual with Chico doing his Hawaiian and Tahitian dancing, the Badjau guests entertained us. Fabiana joined in to dance the *pangalay*, in which slow and sexy movements of the hips are accompanied by graceful movements of the hands, the fingers curved backwards as in Thai and Balinese dancing. The Badjau man stood on his head and moved his legs as if aiming to dance on the ceiling.

The photographer has now rejoined us, but seems too subdued to enter into the spirit of the evening. He has pulled an airline eye-shade over his eyes, and, ignoring the clearing up going on around him, has stretched out on a mat on the floor, going to sleep without so much as a '*buona notte*'.

Chico's purchases had not been good ones. The sail-cloth was much too heavy, and the rope he had bought to supplement the *cabo negro* was too thick. The coil weighed so much that it had been left out on the nearest wooden jetty and would come no nearer to the house before it and the cloth were sent back for exchange.

Good quality bamboo was needed. I had joined Don on a trip down the coast to find some in the forest there, but the quality was not high enough for the outriggers which, acting as floats, had to be large and unblemished by cracks which would allow water to enter and waterlog them. Don volunteered to travel up the coast and to the islands further north-east in the archipelago when a visiting boat returned.

'What? Not gone yet?' we greeted him at 10pm after he had waited all day to leave on the Siasi boat.

'No. *"Mañana"* again,' he replied, unmoved by the delay. Next day he did manage to get away.

Down at the construction site, the S-connectors for the outriggers were being bent from the newly obtained *ligayen*. One end was secured under a heavy fallen tree-trunk, the free end raised over a fulcrum of rock or wood and weights hung on the end. A fire was built under the part of the wood that was to be bent and water was painted over this with an improvised mop every few seconds to soften it.

'Here comes Orphan Annie,' Chico said when he looked up from this work.

'Give us a go with that,' I said, reaching for the mop and continuing the dowsing of the wood.

'Some of The Boys have got hold of a chainsaw and have gone off to cut the steering oar,' he continued conversationally.

'Mmm, soon be away,' I ventured.

'Should be. I sure hope so. I've had enough of *this* damn work already,' Chico said as he returned to the heat of the fire.

The date for leaving was now set for the tenth of April, only two weeks away, and I felt unable to cope with the chaos that would reign before we could get away. The sailing permit for Indonesia had still not been obtained and Bob decided that as soon as Don returned he would have to go to Manila. There was the sail-cloth and rope that had to be changed, and while in the capital perhaps he could also get his knee treated.

The film crew had brought us a Metzler rubber inflatable boat for running around in. It had no board bottom and the underside was covered in rubber patches, like those on a cycle inner tube, which told much of its trip down the Mississippi on the expedition where it had first been used. A ten-horsepower outboard had also been cadged from Tohatsu, and with this Bob and Steve were to journey down to Bongao for the plane.

The night before they left, Bob's pontificating about subjects in my 'expertise' led to another silly confrontation. When he had gone to bed, Chico and I sat up until 4am.

'Underneath that brash façade, he's a pussy cat!' Chico claimed, as I let off steam.

'Well, I wish he'd act like one,' I replied, sulkily.

'Never mind, when they've gone we'll talk properly,' he said, and returned to his hopes and plans for the future. His vulnerability and lack of direction were again apparent.

'Oh, I wish we were through with this expedition,' he broke out. 'I just want to get back to Spain!'

We decided against waiting up for the dawn, and by the time I rose at 6am, Steve had already pumped up the 'Zodiac' and brought it around to the jetty with the forlorn coils of rope on it. They were much too heavy for the rubber ducky and would have to be taken by the next launch that went north. I was sorry that the good-natured Steve would be away for a week or two but looked forward to a break from Bob. Don was not yet back, but Steve and Bob couldn't wait. I would be alone in the house with Chico. Just what I had always wanted . . . but now that the possibility had become reality on a damp, miserable day with the object of my desire snoring on his bed and harbouring even more uncertainties and fears about the expedition than I was, I did not feel so sure.

The rest of the day passed in the usual doctor's rounds and vegetable-collecting trips in the swamp. By the evening we were tired and had letters to write, and the promised heart-to-heart did not materialise. I went early to bed, sorely tempted to invite him too.

'Chico, I'm going to bed now,' I said pointedly.

'Uh? Oh, yeah, sure. Sleep well,' he said, raising his head momentarily from his letter. His reading glasses were perched on the end of his nose, the security string hanging down his bronzed cheek and past the stubble which had replaced the French beard. He smiled distantly, too absorbed in his paper conversations with others to give me much thought.

'Er, Chico?' I quavered.

'Mmm?' like a ruminating cow.

'Er . . .!'

'What?' His curiosity had been pricked a little by my hesitation. Though I had all his attention now, it was still disinterested on a personal level and I lost courage.

'Oh, nothing,' I concluded feebly and went off to struggle my way under my ant-covered mosquito net.

With only two of us to feed, Fabiana was excused the cooking and I displayed my inventiveness, in the frequent absence of fish these days, with a thousand and one ways to make an omelette whenever the chooks granted us a couple of eggs. Freed from Bob's discriminating eye, I experimented in the kitchen and made desserts from overripe bananas and the powdered milk brought on the last supplies run. Chico's response was an assurance that if he did not already have a girlfriend, he would marry me.

The Parrot had been docile and almost well-behaved of late and I began to get worried when he hung his head, did not eat or keep the ants at bay, and was once found hanging by his feet below his perch like a bat. Sometimes he arched his neck and threw his head back in the classic bird symptoms of thiamine deficiency. I voiced my suspicions to Chico that evening,

'I think The Parrot's got beri-beri!'

He suppressed a look of incredulity and pretended to take me seriously.

'How do you know?' He delved for clues on how to handle the situation.

'He's got the signs, and he doesn't get much variety in his diet. There aren't many vitamins in white rice.'

'What can we do about it?' Chico asked, with concern now.

'Give me one of your vitamin pills and we'll try to get a bit down him.'

We took down the poor bird's perch, the ants now crawling over his skin between the bedraggled, damp-looking feathers. With a healthy 'The Parrot', this would have been a painful and dangerous experience for us, but he didn't have the strength to bite. We placed him and the perch in a box which we suspended from a wire across the room, but the ants soon cracked the problem of getting to that. Next day I put the box on a chair and placed all four legs in water.

I would have liked to try out a vitamin B1 tablet to find out if it really was this nutrient he lacked, but Chico took his vitamins comprehensively and only multi-vitamin 'gob-stoppers' were available.

'Perhaps it's as well for The Parrot, if not for my scientific curiosity,' I thought, as I spooned the dissolved pill into his beak while Chico held him gently but firmly. When next I dosed him in this way I added some sugar and powdered clapperboard chalk for good measure.

A few days later, cleaning The Parrot's box had become so dangerous that I pronounced the patient well enough to be returned to his perch.

('So you nearly became an ex-parrot,' Steve mimicked as we replaced him later, moving the perch so that journeys to the shower could be taken with greater safety.)

Don returned after ten days away, bringing with him a packet of pork cooked in ginger and aniseed. Chico had been getting worried about him and was glad to have him back. I liked his company too, but realised I had missed my one chance to get close to Chico. After that first evening I had hoped to pluck up courage again but the discovery of a cache of letters for us on a launch which had docked the week before made letter writing a continuous occupation and most communication was limited to the written word.

With Don back, we began to talk in the evenings. I had enjoyed being together with Chico in silence but was thirsting for stimulating and refreshing conversation. But I was disappointed here too. I did not seem to be on the same wavelength when they talked philosophically, and kept silent as I knew they would think the conversation was above my head.

Sometimes talk turned to practical matters, and Don was as discomfited as I by Chico's dismissal of my chief worry – how we were to carry enough water for our journey over the Indian Ocean.

'Hell! What about the boat? If that's not made right we'll all drown anyway!' Chico countered, almost as illogical as Bob in his dismissal of one problem just because there was a greater one to worry about. If this was the sort of response I was to get to all those 'questions I wasn't asking', I did not intend to ask any more.

I mentioned Bob's scatterbrained way of doing things and was assured that he had the 'intention' that something would be achieved and it somehow always arranged itself in the end.

Now we don't want any personality rivalries on this trip,' Chico cautioned us both.

'Sure, I'm not going to complain about anything that can't be changed,' Don replied.

'Me neither,' I joined in, hurt by Chico's feeling the need to tell us what we had the intelligence to realise, that dissent could jeopardise the success of the expedition.

Chico considered himself a palmist and he read our hands.

'I've got a long life ahead of me,' he stated, on the basis of his long lifeline when he told his own fortune.

'Great! I'll stick with you then, Chico,' Don said.

'So will I. We won't get shipwrecked with you around!' I agreed.

Next morning, I walked up the hill overlooking the boat-building site. Crouching down to gaze at the beautiful, continuous blue of sky and sea that lightened from royal to azure at the horizon, I began to cry. Being miserable in cold, rainy, urban ugliness is defensible, but here, in this lovely setting which many a winter-bound Briton would envy me, guilt sharpened my misery.

I was here as a nutritionist, but had no food on which to work and little specialised knowledge, and felt unworthy of a part in this adventure. I dreaded a voyage of drudgery in the galley but that seemed the only course to take. I still suffered from too much attention from Bob and too little from Chico. I would rather die than miss the voyage, but I already wanted to get away from these people.

Our comfortable threesome lasted only a couple of days. Bob and Steve returned on a rainy afternoon with Kirsten (Kiki), a German freelance journalist. There were more people in Bongao waiting for room on the inflatable.

It was good to see Steve, who was as cheery as ever, but almost voiceless after living it up in the 'big city'. Bob was also renewed by the change of scene.

'How are you, Sal?' he roared with pleasure at being home again.

'All the better for a few days without me, eh?' he ventured, and I smiled at his honesty and generosity of spirit. He was probably a lot happier for the break from me too. I determined (again) to be more understanding of the strain he was undergoing.

'Anything interesting happen while we were away, Chico?' he enquired.

'Oh, just a deputation saying the men haven't been paid for getting the *ligayen* two months ago. José's acting kinda strange, too. There were some funny goings-on out there with the Taiwanese junks. We think they've made a run for it. Sally found a live rat in her bed one night. Oh, and The Parrot's had . . . er . . . beri-beri, is it?' he consulted me.

'Did we miss anything?' Steve enquired, coming in with the same priorities as Bob.

'Nahhh!' Bob answered for us. 'Same old nine-to-five grind.'

Bob was in good form and kept us amused for a long time with his tales from the hospital. They had admitted him and shaved his injured leg and half-way up his chest in preparation for an exploratory operation, but fearing that the surgery could take weeks to heal, he escaped and consulted a traditional healer instead. The comical way in which he described his return to hospital with medicinal leaves slipping from the bandage concealed the worry he must have felt. We were due to sail in a few days and the captain was still an invalid.

At dinner Bob returned to the discussion of whether José should come with us to Madagascar. When the suggestion had first been made, I had jumped at the opportunity of having someone else to cook; but now that I knew him better I considered the prospect of being the chef preferable to suffering José's sly subservience.

I was concerned lest my dislike of him should be construed as racism. The crew so far were all Westerners and it would be good to have an Asian along. It was a pity though that the one who had the skill to be of use and the time to come along should be the one we were less than charmed by. Chico did not really want him either, Steve kept his prudent silence as usual, and Don, who was better able to admire a person for their skill and suppress any feelings about personality, said it was a good idea. Bob liked to have a show of democracy among the crew members, but ultimately the decision was his, and José was asked to join us.

The next afternoon was threatening rain when Steve arrived back with Albrecht Schaefer, another German journalist who lived in the Philippines, and Smiley (Steven Aubrey), an Australian friend of Steve's who had come to join the crew. He was tall and skinny, though we soon found he could eat prodigiously, and the only born Australian on the crew. It was obvious how he had got his nickname. He looked benevolently about him, but with a certain timidity not usually associated with men of his nationality.

Albrecht, fair and balding, was amiable and quiet, almost apologetic in his interrogations, but I presumed he had a more aggressive side since he seemed to be a successful journalist.

Early the next morning, Steve and I took Albrecht and Kiki to Bongao in the rubber inflatable to catch their plane. I had no special duties, but since I had been almost three months in this quiet place without a break, one night in the metropolis was to be my reward.

Chico had obviously taken a great liking to Kiki and I burned with jealousy and resented the freedom a short-term visitor enjoyed. I tried not to see when Chico bent down to the boat to kiss her goodbye, then we were away, bouncing over the choppy water, Albrecht holding the painter rope as if riding a bucking bronco. His wooden seat was over a box and there was a strangled cry when he momentarily trapped his nether organs between the two. Steve made a sympathetic attempt to make the ride less bumpy, whilst at the same time aware of the need to reach the airport in time.

They waded ashore near the seaside runway, watched by those bemused passengers already waiting to board. Up to our knees in the sea, we exchanged goodbyes, and Kiki gave me money to buy a few beers for Chico's birthday.

'Give him a kiss for me!' she called back over her shoulder.

'I sure will!' I cried enthusiastically.

After three months in a village of pedestrians, the bumbling progress of the cars we met on our walk into town seemed like breakneck speed to me, and I experienced something of the culture shock of the peasant going to the city for the first time – though this was hardly Brooklyn. We checked into the Southern Hotel, which did not live down to my expectations after the tales I had heard of its squalor. It seemed to be the only hotel around and was, therefore, where the action was. As we ate our restaurant meal downstairs we observed the many transvestite prostitutes chatting up customers. I found it strange that in a society where we had found it better to book into one hotel room (with two single beds) as Mr and Mrs Corrigan, such unorthodox sexual behaviour was tolerated much better than in our own.

Even by day we saw men walking openly with make-up on, and as we passed the hairdresser's owned by a group of elegant homosexuals, I waved at the cordial crowd. Perhaps they considered themselves as my fellow females and treated me accordingly, but to Steve they must have been sending out sexual signals and tacit invitations.

'Oh look! *Do* be friendly,' I urged. 'I think they're beautiful, don't you?' I taunted him innocently.

'Huh!' was all he could bring himself to utter.

The long-awaited night on a mattress was wasted in sleeplessness, and we strolled over to the dingy café across the road for unaccustomed coffee and cakes. This was my first sight of a Philippine town, apart from Manila, and here too life seemed to have been affected by 'three hundred years in a Spanish convent and fifty years of Hollywood'. I was struck by the almost imperceptible dovetailing of American culture into the older way of life in some things, and their stark separation elsewhere. Billboards bore familiar American faces advertising toothpaste, for example, but were written in Tagalog. The main store in town looked modern, as did the petrol station, while the traditional houses and muddy market seemed never to have been touched by a Western thought.

Returning to Languyan from the waterside market with a few ceramics, I was pleased to have had this outing, but I preferred my calm village people to this maelstrom of mendicants and merchants. I was not sorry to be returning to our rural home after only twenty-four hours away.

The journey back proved to be a wild, rough ride, during which all but one of the ceramic pots we had wrapped so carefully were broken and discarded over the side. We arrived, soaked through and exhausted, to find the others had been slaving over the sail canvas all morning, with the sun beating down on them. The new, finer cloth was cut and spread on the south-facing slope beside the Teahouse and we soon learnt the particular stitch we were to employ to seam, hem and sew on the bolt rope at the edges. Even wearing hats, the heat made us dizzy and nauseous, and the rain showers now were a blessing. After the evening meal we went out again to sew until 10pm, small pools of light from the pressure lamps illuminating the work and attracting villagers and soldiers from the military post behind who helped desultorily as they pursued their life's work of fraternal communication.

The sails were soon finished and we all set to work on the deck. Split lengths of bamboo were tied to the wooden pole framework which projected out over the outriggers on each side. The binding was rattan, which was in short supply, and the constant cause of negotiations with people who knew where to find it in the forest. I now discovered what really hard work was like; the sun beating down without mercy, and the crick in the back and neck increasing as I took my turn below the growing deck, threading the rattan strand back up to the weaver above. Our palms and fingers were soon criss-crossed with cuts as we pulled tight the narrow edges of the rattan, but here at last was satisfying work directly on the craft.

On Easter Sunday, it was Chico's birthday. We drank Kiki's beer and I delivered her kiss, surprising Chico who had thought I was man-shy. Next day, Bob and Chico went up the coast to fetch the *imam* from Ungusan. The *Sarimanok* was almost completed and we needed the holy man for the blessing ceremony. The sleeping cabin was now ready on the boat, and Bob had already installed himself in his berth there so the Muslim 'priest' could sleep on his bed in the house.

The evening's tranquillity was marred by the constant drone of the *imam* reading out loud to himself. He settled on Bob's bed early and slept oblivious of the light and the readers at the table. As I passed by to the other room I noticed that his rifle lay beside him on the bed. I could see that a through-the-floorboard job would have to suffice for any calls of nature that night, a dunny-run past a fearful, armed man being decidedly unwise.

The morning ceremony was to be filmed, but the holy man did not realise what this entailed and had to be restrained from beginning his Arabic prayers before we were ready. A verse from the Koran, sewn into a piece of cloth, was lodged under the main mast before which the ceremony took place, and another was hidden inside the cabin where the captain would not find it, as prescribed by the *imam*.

The local ship builders were dressed in their best sarongs and they sat at ease on deck as they listened to the foreign but familiar words. The ceremony culminated in the beheading of a chicken and scattering of blood about the mast, the mortal body of the bird being craftily snaffled afterwards by an avaricious shopkeeper.

After the party that followed, Smiley, Steve and I took the *imam* back to his village. The man sat stock still with his gun pointed skyward beside him. When it started to rain he was offered a large plastic bag to cover himself – he promptly wrapped it around his armalite and sat stolidly getting soaked without complaint, content that his valued possession was safe.

During the return journey Steve stopped the boat and cut the motor to sniff the air and enjoy the breeze. He worked in Australia as a sailing master for a rich yacht owner, and sailing was his passion.

'This wind is perfect for our trip,' he announced with a satisfied sigh. 'Ahhh! Let me at it! This is what I've come for!'

All hands were now working for our release. José was making a bilge pump and Chico went out at night to do the caulking, spending so long away that we forgot him and he had to wake someone to let him in. I was asked to 'skin the onions' in the sack, which seemed a peculiar thing to do if they were to be kept for weeks, but I did not question my captain's commands. I had almost finished cutting off all the papery outer leaves to expose the flesh before Bob noticed and put me right.

'That's not it,' he said calmly. 'Look. Just rub off the outer leaves with your hands so they won't get into the bilge and clog up the pump,' and he demonstrated with one of the few remaining intact corms.

'Looks as though I've been wasting my time then,' I said, crestfallen.

'Yes,' he said simply, and hurried to get on with his other work. I was a fool, and on this occasion he knew that I knew it and did not rub it in, but his self-restraint heaped coals of fire on my head.

I felt that I blundered again when some wood needed to be ferried from a local store to the hold, and I found myself incapable of even the simple job of peddling the *banka* to the jetty. My impotence against the power of the wind and tide even in that sheltered creek was frightening. I re-tied at my starting place, and looked around warily to make sure my efforts were not being mocked, then stomped up the hill to get help like the weakling female I was. When all was said and done, the only thing I was good for was being the cook, and I was not very good for that.

Bob was ecstatic at the sensitivity of the steering of the *Sarimanok* on our first sea trial, though gybing (turning the sail around to follow a different tack) was a Herculean task with the heavy bamboo booms. We all took a turn at the tiller, and I climbed up the ladder part of the tripod main mast as we returned up the creek to V.G.'s house to show off the finished product.

Things moved fast now. The house, no longer repaired whenever a new hole appeared in the floor or roof and left to the mercy of the exploding rat population, was finally ransacked for everything we needed on board with no respect shown to the place that had been home a couple of hours before. Some local people demonstrated equal indifference to us by not waiting for us to depart the village before they dismantled the beds they had been promised. These now stood forlorn under a roof denuded of the best nipa, taken to cover our cabin shelter.

After a chaotic morning, fraught and tense from the usual recriminations, I gave up my hopeless attempt to catch the last of our chickens, thanked the termite-killed mango tree for refraining from falling on our house before we left, and skudded down the hill to board the *Sarimanok*. Antonio, who had become unpredictable and nervous as the job came to an end, had gone home to Zamboanga, and Fabiana had departed for the mainland days ago, taking our trashy novels and The Parrot to sell. The last remaining Boys had caught the Siasi boat that morning, so the glance and 'goodbye' that V.G.'s secretary and a few others cast our way as we departed was the nearest we got to a send-off. Two and a half months and eight hours late, we were away.

Part two
And all who sail in her

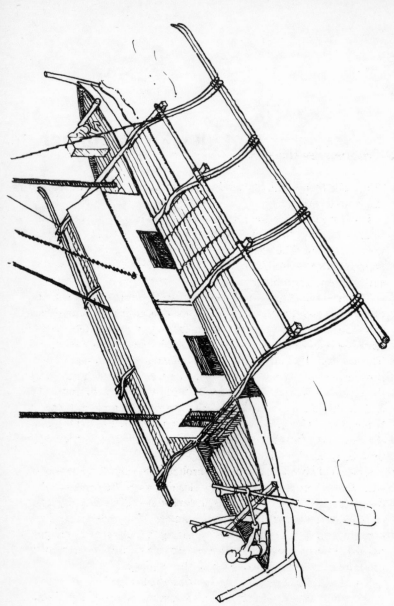

Sarimanok at the start of the journey in 1984

5. Troubles by the yard

'Shit. The bloody thing's coming straight for us!' Bob yelled. 'Get the lamp lit quick!'

Don fumbled with the pressure lamp which shed the brightest illumination but took some skill to light. We prayed he would get it right first time as we watched the red port- and the green starboard-light getting closer. The huge ship was bearing down at speed on our small boat.

'Got it!' Don panted, and the bright light threw a small sphere of visibility about him. The white globe danced from side to side as he climbed the widely spaced rungs to the top of the mast, leaving us below in darkness again until the smaller lamps could be lit. The glow on which we were depending seemed to contract as the substance of the boat that it revealed tapered to a point formed by the three wooden poles of the mast. With it our hope diminished and we realised what a feeble beacon this was. Having nothing better, Don held up the heavy lamp from his perch at the top of the mast and swung it in a pendulum arc, changing arms frequently until both were aching.

The small outboard motor had broken down and there was no wind for sail propulsion. We were sloshing about helplessly in the deep water between Mindanao and Sulawesi and invisible by sight or radar to the vessels that plied the waters. The port-light had come into view first as Steve was repairing the motor by torchlight, but when the starboard was noticed also, we went into emergency procedure as we now lay directly in the ship's path.

'Oh God, I hope there's somebody on the bridge!'

'I bet he's only looking at the radar screen,' someone piped up, knowing that a wooden boat would be undetected that way.

It was useless to shout, the steamer's engine noise would drown that and, with his attention trained on the navigational instruments rather than on the sea, the pilot could easily overlook us. Our wooden boat would be crumpled to matchwood, unnoticed.

As soon as we sailed away from Tawi Tawi, the wind, whose every flicker and change of direction on land had been monitored with fluctuating glee or despair, now showed us it was not going to cooperate. The plan had been that we sail around the north of Tawi Tawi, go south-east to the east of Sulawesi, and travel down the Moluccas with frequent stops before turning west and sailing along the eastern islands of Indonesia to Bali. Once there, we would get ready for The Big One, that is the non-stop crossing of the Indian Ocean to Madagascar.

There was no south-westerly wind for the outset so we had to rely immediately on the small outboard motor mounted on a rig slung from the stern *batangan* to get us to our last two stops in Mindanao. The two masts stood bare, awaiting their turn to serve. The outriggers rested gently on the water, one on each side of the hull. With the bamboo deck extended towards them, the craft really must have looked like the raft of legend in the 'Erythrean Sea'.

The bow and stern were decked up to the level of the gunwales and for the first half hour I sat on the tapering bow and straddled the *pamalong*, hugging it as if riding a giraffe with my arms around its neck, and gazed at the smooth water under the bow. With bare feet dangling over that slipping stream of water, I felt the liberty of a bareback rider in the wilds and was unmoved by the furore of the distant, noisy squabbling of seas birds as they dived repeatedly to massacre a shoal of fish below the surface.

I could have dreamed there for hours if Steve had not called me to the steering oar at the port quarter of the stern. I sat on the deck, here also flush with the gunwale, and placed my lower legs in the sunken part just in front, so that my feet rested on the strip of lowered deck. Here too one was close to the water both vertically and horizontally, and I reflected that wakefulness was advisable as a sleeper could literally 'drop off' into the sea.

The cabin occupied the centre of the canoe over the hull. The deck over the outrigger supports also extended a short way into the cabin as four approximately six-foot berths, two head-to-toe down each side. These were too short for Don and Bob to be comfortable, and lying full length I too found my feet pressed to the thick thwart bounding the sleeping spaces and occasionally rested in the berth below my shelf, my feet thrust between the rope lashings. These lower sleeping spaces were gloomy by day and more secluded from lights at night, but they were just at sea level and water seeped in between the planks. The upper ones were less claustrophobic and were only infrequently washed by a wave. Shutters covered large 'windows', one beside each bunk. Since they were usually tied open, they made more convenient doors than the doorways at each end. It also made me feel safer to have an opening beside me in case the boat should turn turtle – an accident these 'trimarans' were prone to.

José was already working at the fire box, a ridiculously tall hut like a public convenience, which at first perched on the deck at the bow, forming a second horn behind the high stempiece to this seeming rhinoceros' snout. It then moved for a while to the starboard deck, but with all the equipment needed for the cooking on that side, the boat was unbalanced and it still made a mockery of the aerodynamics. It found its final niche backing on to the forward part of the cabin, whose height was also a source of annoyance to the captain, presenting, as it did, such a large resistance to the air.

Steve's often perfunctory performance of duties on land had been transformed into precise, unceasing graft as soon as we had cast off and he hardly looked up from his tasks, except briefly to scan the horizon, until landfall was imminent. I recovered from my piqued resentment of the world in general when a few peaceful minutes of this sedate pace lulled me into a better temper. I acquitted myself quite well at the helm and rejoiced silently that I had stuck out my long, bitter probationary period on land.

Land was never out of sight that first day and, when the port of Tumbagaan was reached at nightfall, the approach through the rocky shallows was negotiated with care.

'Oh, look at those lovely boats!' I exclaimed on seeing large double-outrigger canoes with central masts streaming evenly radiating ropes like maypole ribbons from their summit.

'Yes. They're *basnigan*. The cables support the outriggers on each side,' Bob informed me. 'They're used a lot round here.'

We stopped for the night and I lay out under the stars until the gnawing of the single rat we found we had on board, and the heavy mist which dampened my blanket and pearled the deck with drew drops, sent me inside around midnight.

Early rising was necessary to complete one's morning functions before it was light enough to be embarrassed by the curious eyes always watching from shore. The red ensign I had brought from London was tied to the stern *pamalong* and by mid-morning we were underway again.

We were bound for another small island where we hoped to get petrol. It now seemed certain we would be able to sail very little on the way to Bali and we had to stock up on fuel. The channel through the shallows at Tabawan was visible ahead to someone scanning from the mast, but a false move brought *Sari* to a standstill with the hull on the bottom. As we waited for high tide, Don and Bob snorkelled and popped up from time to time with reports on the sea life, which I lazily investigated from my prostrate position on the deck, peering over the edge to the coral bottom.

Tabawan is built over the sea with catwalks between. Walking through this wooden Venice for the first time in the dark, we needed guidance to and from any destination, but we found it even more frightening the next day when the safety net of the sea had fled, leaving the sea bed exposed far below the lacey walkways.

The bowline broke in the night and the splash woke us to the sight of the boat crushing its own outrigger by pressing beam-on to another vessel, a kind of self-mutilation she was often to try in the next three months. The shouting and running around that was necessary to save and re-tie her was also to become horribly familiar before we reached Bali.

The morrow was for errands, renewing our petrol supplies and searching for drinking water.

'Why don't we just take some that this lady's offering, Sally?' Don enquired, as a fragile old woman put her meagre resources at our disposal.

'Oh, it's very nice of her, but it looks oily, and look there are mosquito larvae in it,' I observed, as a prod at the surface of the uncovered oil drum sent hundreds of tiny worm-like animals into paroxisms of squirming to escape to the dark depths. It was hard to refuse politely so generous an offer, but freedom from mosquitoes and flies was one of the lures of the open sea, and I was not going to stand for insect stowaways.

To avoid another wait in the exit channel, we stayed overnight to catch the morning high tide. The bright lights beckoned, and Chico and Bob were soon entertaining people in an outdoor bar with their renditions of homegrown music.

The Hawaiian language seems to be full of vowels separated by glottal stops, with scarcely a hard consonant to nail it to familiarity. Chico sang Hawaiian songs, accompanied on the ukelele that appeared on request. The effect on the ring of people of all ages that gathered around was electric. They laughed a while then quietened themselves and shushed neighbours to listen again to find if the strange sounds were true, then burst out again in derision at the *Milikan* jabbering as if trying to cool something in his mouth which was burning his tongue.

These people were not yokels. Many dressed and wore their hair like city dwellers and were aware of the wide world, even though they continued to live on this remote isle. At least, it seemed remote to me, being used to a much larger island where any town without a road to it is virtually inaccessible. They had the seaways, however, and were easier to visit than a bedouin camp far into the desert, as long as you had the transport. How lucky I was to have happened upon the means of getting to such places, I thought. On evenings like this, I could hardly believe that I was here.

Consultations with knowledgeable people in the village convinced Bob that it was foolhardy to try to push against the wind with our small motor to get to the Moluccas. The wind would be right on the nose and our best course would be to pass down the Makassar Straits between Sulawesi and Borneo. This way we could reach Bali in plenty of time to catch the June and July south-east trade winds across the ocean before they became too strong, and learn how to sail this ancient-style craft in the process. We were disappointed not to be going to the 'Spice Islands', but the ultimate objective was Madagascar, and any desires that conflicted with reaching our goal had to be jettisoned. The next day, after a struggle to get *Sari* off a sandbank, we headed south with a school of dolphins. We had left the Philippines at last.

My watch was from eight to twelve, morning and night, with Bob. It was advantageous to be on watch with the captain since sail changes were most likely then and those not on watch would be called up to help. Poor Chico and Don now had the dreadful twelve to four watch – brain-bakingly hot by day, and inconveniently placed in the middle of the night when little sleep could be enjoyed either before or after. Their first night's nap was broken, as was Steve's and Smiley's, when the winds were fair enough – aft of the beam (from somewhere behind for the non-nautical) – for the engine to be abandoned in favour of the sails.

The heavy main had to be hauled by an enormous effort, with all the men trying to get a grip on the one rope. Later a second halyard was added, which enabled more people to pull effectively. Pulleys were not used in the days of the migrations so similar structures, without the rotating wheel, were made. These 'dead eyes', fashioned from blocks of wood carried for repairs and alterations, smoothed the passage of the rope through the highest point up the mast where they were hung.

No sooner was the sail raised than the bamboo yard (the pole supporting the sail at the top) broke with a sickening crack, and the weight of the canvas brought the ends of the fibrous tube down with a creaking sound of splintering xylem as of a falling tree. After some minutes to digest the implications of that setback, the mizzen was raised, but it would not set right and was lowered again. The mizzen mast seemed to be too far back and a sail there played havoc with the steering. I returned to the tiller of a boat again powered by the sputtering, noisy motor, and enjoyed an hour or two of comfortable navigation by the stars on the clear night.

We had a compass for this part of the voyage, but once the heading was established, it was preferable to keep to it by fixing a particular star or cloud in relation to a mast rung, for instance, and keeping it there for a while, consulting the compass only periodically to readjust the direction and perhaps choose another star when the constellations had moved over a little.

Spare bamboo was kept aboard for emergencies, and on the following day one piece was laced on to the sail as a new yard. It didn't even make its debut on the mast, however, as one end dipped momentarily into the sea at the forward end of the outrigger deck and the weight of water which filled the trailing canvas swept it back under the *Sarimanok*'s wing as we moved over the surface, and broke it in seconds. The break was not central, so the bamboo could be recycled as a shorter boom (stiffening rod on the bottom of the sail), but the unwieldiness of our ancient equipment, and the poor quality of the bamboo, was chastening to our spirits.

Everyone's sleep was broken that same night with another sail hoist during my watch and I hoped that the wind would hold out this time so that the men who were up and working throughout the day would get some proper rest.

When our watch hours were first assigned to us, I saw I was bracketed with José, which obviously augured a sharing of cooking duties too. I scotched that little set-up before we even left home, saying 'I'd rather die' than be the little woman in a support role on this voyage and miss all the real satisfaction of sailing the boat. If José was coming after all, he could do the cooking. He liked the work and I did not, so why complicate matters with rotas?

Bob let me off with the observation that they would probably starve if they relied on me to feed them, at which Chico gave him a sharp look and hazarded a protest, having found that I could do quite well when not pummelled by confidence-sapping witticisms. Perhaps being considered incapable is better than any excuse, however, and I let the calumny pass.

José was good with the fire and squatted uncomplaining at his task for most of the day, battling with the added difficulties of cooking on a gently rocking seesaw. He could not be expected to wash up as well, however, and a rota was soon devised for the rest of us. With most people washing their own clothes, except when I did a few for the others to make up for the lighter duties I performed as the weakest crew member, we were soon rubbing along quite well.

Watches could be pleasant on warm nights with no problems, sitting talking to Bob. We sailed frequently enough for me, a new sailor, to master the art of keeping the wind in the sails. This vessel could not sail with the wind much forward of the beam, while the slightest yaw from the chosen direction could cause the wind to get in front of the sail and pin it back on the mast with a bang of bamboo on wood, the canvas billowing on either side of the pole like a pair of granny's bloomers. This happened to me on the third night and Bob raced back to the helm to point it out (unnecessarily).

'Did you lose concentration for a moment?' he asked kindly, giving me a feasible explanation for the error to cling to.

'No. It's so hard to keep dead straight. I kept sweeping from side to side, then she went too far,' I explained.

'You must have lost concentration,' he tried again to make me admit to daydreaming on duty.

'No. I said it just swung round too close to the wind and the wind got in front of the sail,' I persisted stubbornly with the truth.

'You lost concentration!' he stated categorically now, as if he had not heard what I said.

'I didn't, I . . .'

'Never mind, put it right!' he commanded, and I reached for the lower sheet (rope tied to the edges or corners of the sail with which its set can be manipulated). The one to my right (starboard) was just within reach and I pulled it towards me so that the luff (the edge nearer the wind which was the port side here) would move forward with the fulcrum of the mast and the wind would be once again behind it.

'Don't pull the sail like that,' Bob ordered.

'But that's how I've seen it done by the others,' I said and tried again.

Both our voices were raised now.

'You stupid girl. Get this boat back on course!' he roared at me, without giving instructions, bawling at me again when I tried the only method I knew. His illogicality and injustice overpowered me with such hatred that I trembled and almost fainted with the intensity of it.

'You'd better do it yourself, then,' I was about to fling at him, when he had the same thought himself and asked me, quite calmly, to get out of the cockpit which he then entered to impress me with the mastery of his sailing technique.

Despite my upset, I stopped to watch and learn how the job should be done, and once he was sitting in control he reached for the starboard sheet and yanked it towards him until the leading edge of the sail conquered the gust attacking it from in front and billowed forward as it was blown from behind. In other words, he did exactly what he had prevented me from doing. Once we were sailing well again, he returned the helm to me, without a hint of apology. As soon as he was out of earshot, I sobbed uncontrollably, making plans to jump overboard.

Don told me later he had heard what went on and I know that others were sometimes bawled at, justly or not I cannot tell, but rather than wasting sleeping time on thoughts of sympathy, I would snuggle down selfishly on my bunk and feel glad it was someone else that was suffering. I think there is something about sailing which brings out the tyrannical side of a person's nature and conquers reserves of tolerance for the less experienced or skilled. A sort of sadism comes to the surface, too, where normal comforts, even if available, are not to be partaken of by the tyrant or her/his underlings who, no matter how free from seasickness or how stout in the face of danger, will always remain 'land-lubbers' to the despot. I privately labelled this the 'Captain Bligh Syndrome'.

Even my pal Steve was transformed at sea. He worked well and continuously, but gave commands into the wind which could not be heard, or used nautical language I had not yet acquired and blamed me when the commands were not carried out. Rather than translate into plain English, the command was repeated over and over, progressively louder and more slowly as if I was a stupid foreigner who *must* be able to understand English really if I only tried hard enough. To be fair, Steve sometimes taught me words, knots and general nautical practice, but he rarely had time and, though I learnt the language by observing the 'natives', I never became fluent.

After breakfast the sail was hoisted again and the yard promptly broke. It was repaired there and then and rehoisted, only to break again within the hour. The third and fourth raising that day were comparatively easy for the muscle men since Bob eliminated the problem by omitting the troublesome stiffening boom, and later the yard also. We looked like a Viking longboat now, with sheets taut as bowstrings pinioning the corners. The wind was directly astern and the sails set parallel to the beam as in the ancient square-riggers.

That day, Don pointed out a whale in the distance, which as usual I failed to see. Being a little shortsighted, I was impressed that the others were able to train their gaze so far. The surface of the boat and a few yards of sea were all that I was usually aware of except when I was busy lassoing stars and clouds for navigational purposes. When I did just stop and look, I was suddenly aware of the stupidity of our bustle and worry when so much peace and beauty lay all round. Even when the sea was choppy, its uniformity as far as the eye could see was somehow tranquillising.

The flexibility of our strange vessel enabled it to withstand a battering that would crack a more rigid structure, but the constantly changing levels of the side decks, as the two outriggers rode up and down over waves independently, caused the two back supports to the main mast to work on each other and on the upright and to loosen the rope that bound them. The supports passed through the cabin roof to the thick centre thwart and made the whole place writhe, letting in water on to sleeping faces when it rained at night. Another structural worry to be dealt with before The Big One.

Bob felt that square-rigging was unethical on a boat which demanded a different kind of sail, and soon the repaired yards and booms, split lengths of bamboo coating the bent and splintery parts of the broken ones for strength, were relaced on to the sail which was mounted again. During our night watch, the reinforced yard broke once more and the exhausted sailors were winkled out to take down the sail again.

Back with the faithful workhorse (or nine-point-nine horses as the outboard's power was supposed to equate), I was left alone at the helm. Secure in the knowledge that I could not back the sails, or be heard above the drone of the motor, I revelled in the effective solitude and entertained myself to an amalgamated Christmas and Easter service (the best kind with music only), throwing back my head and singing my favourite carols and hymns, while following a bright star in the south.

Before an awning to shade the helmsman (or woman) was set up next day, I cooled my time on the tiller by a resumption of the carolling.

In the bleak mid winter,
Frosty wind made moan,
Earth stood hard as iron,
Water like a stone.

I had always thought the choice of such a hymn an act of malice on the part of the chorister, since, though it was musically pleasing, the vivid references to bitter cold were bound to increase the misery of children shivering in unheated stone buildings or contemplating the first school period of netball on an icy court, but here and now its words were wonderfully refrigerating.

Wind and consequent sail changes dogged our next day and night, and the rain found a way under my super-duper Giltex all-in-one sailing suit by sheer perseverance. The material of the garment was wonderful but the seams were its undoing (in a manner of speaking), and the reason Steve sometimes sported a scarf became obvious. It resulted in a sopping chin and neck but kept the liquid from trickling down to the belly button.

Estimating our position by dead-reckoning using the conventional methods of sextant readings, Steve warned we were getting too close to Borneo, and we veered east again to Sulawesi, where we needed to stop for more bamboo. The engine had been going continuously for days and, went on strike for better conditions. This stretch of water just north of Sulawesi must have been a shipping channel and, while Steve strove to make the motor see reason, the steamer came into view ploughing a furrow through the sea straight towards us.

Some minutes after doing all we could to advertise our presence, there were no visible signs that our warning had been heeded. The red and green demonic 'eyes' were still trained in our direction and the tanker's engine noise became louder, like mood music in a horror film, building up tension and foreboding irrespective of the commonplace nature of the visuals. Don must have been almost falling from the mast with exhaustion and the rest of us stood redundant below, hopping from foot to foot with frustration at our inability to do anything, when the green light was slowly extinguished from our sight and we knew the vessel had swerved north.

The intimidating noise of the monster came nearer and nearer, though it had changed pitch, indicating the vessel had also reduced speed, and in a few moments it passed a few yards off our stern. We looked up at the metal hull as far as the light allowed as if at a cliff face from the foot. The steersman had seen us and taken action to avoid a collision and then, as if having inspected our boat and decided we needed no further notice, he revved up the engine again and disappeared into the darkness.

The rest of the night was bound to be an anticlimax, but the disrupted and more frequently changing watches meant only snatches of sleep for everyone, interspersed by two-hour long vigils of anxiously scanning the horizon for lights. The *Sarimanok*, suspended by its own buoyancy over fathoms of water, spun in leisurely pirouettes, first clockwise then anticlockwise, intelligence of the movement in the featureless sea revealed to the eyes by the wheeling constellations overhead.

'Just sit down here on the *batangan* and look all round every few minutes,' Chico advised when my lonely watch began, and I sat on the thick wooden beam near the open shutter beside his bed. I felt safer for having him nearby, even if he was asleep, and the fact that I was not tramping about the boat and risking falling overboard unnoticed – the greatest hazard on this boat – allowed him to relax. Soon, however, I found the best place for watching comfortably was sitting cross-legged on top of the cabin roof like a garden gnome, which gave Chico a few bad moments when he awoke and found me gone.

I wore my glasses on watch since it was important to see well, but peered hard and long out to sea all around me more frequently than necessary, and was often shocked to see a light where there had been none before only to find it was a glow I had recently identified as a star on my left which now appeared behind me as the boat had spun around.

Chico's forthright style of sailing finished off another yard next day but he escaped with only a mild tongue-lashing from Bob as we returned once again to the repaired motor for power. Sulawesi must be close by now and Steve tried to pinpoint the town of Dondo. The night time brought the northern coast into reach and a forgotten smell came to our nostrils.

'Aah! Get a whiff of that!' Bob exclaimed in rapturous recognition, as of a longlost love.

'*Kretek* ciggies. We must be very near Indonesia now!' he cried joyously.

Our accession to the first goal on our route could not have been more aptly and unmistakably marked. Perhaps because of our poor powers of discrimination between subtly different odours, scent is more evocative of time and place than stimulation of any of our more highly developed senses, and the pungent smell of these distinctive clove cigarettes exclusive to Indonesia makes them inseparable from memories of the country.

Voices became audible then as the Indonesian fishermen smoked and chatted over their work. Bob called out to them in *Bahasa Indonesia*.

'Hey, please can you help us? Which way to Dondo?' The stunned silence attendant on hearing a foreign voice in such a place took on a new quality when the men saw what a weird boat the foreigners were sailing.

'Let's get up close and speak to them,' Bob suggested and soon two small double-outrigger canoes were tied nose-on to our mighty *katig* and Bob, clad in salmon-coloured canvas sailing jacket and white trousers, walked barefoot down an outrigger arm to greet them. Ducking his lofty brow to the level of their shelter, he pleaded our case politely until an adventurous fisherman climbed with agility up the same *batangan* to the deck and pored with Steve and Bob over the chart. He now seemed unimpressed by this unusual late-night phenomenon and pointed out the route on the charts with the self-assurance of a veteran instructing his wide-eyed pupils. We were directed east along the coast and even led some of the way to the nearest large town. Watches were disrupted again and I saw the rosy dawning of a clear day over the hills of Sulawesi.

The national flag had to be flown now.

'Oh damn! I can't remember which goes on top, the red or the white,' Bob mused, wrinkling his brow in an effort of recall.

'You've been there, Sal. Don't you remember?'

'Red on top feels more right, somehow,' I considered and he agreed, so I climbed with trepidation up the mast to fix the flag there. The strange motion of the boat was rarely smooth, with each outrigger in turn rising a little then slapping the sea on its descent as its partner rose to gather momentum to display the same fit of temper. The mast therefore not only swayed unnervingly but jolted and juddered at each side of its sky-scraping arch, making imprudent any use of the hands except for holding on. The others managed all right, however, so I boldly followed their example, only to be mortified when Chico later found it necessary to ascend to tie the flag higher and better.

Personal preparations for our first step on to Indonesian soil were also underway. Steve foamed his face ready for a shave before the sextant mirror posed on the cabin roof, and then joined the rest of us in tidying up the slovenliness into which our possessions had deteriorated in only five nights at sea. Things were stuffed into the racks above the bunks which were as spacious as those on coaches or trains, so high was our cabin. Though not quite high enough for anyone, even José, to stand upright under the summit of the sloping roof, it should really be reduced considerably before the ocean voyage.

We glided over glassy smooth water, into the harbour of Toli Toli, where another smell greeted us. It was the sickly sweet smell of dried coconut flesh, copra, emanating from a drying and sacking factory on the water front. It was pleasant at first, but after a few days of the continuous reek, my liking for coconut waned.

Bob was already dressed in his respectable clothes by the time we docked beside a passenger ship crammed with people ogling us from each deck. He got straight down to the business of presenting our passports to the authorities, and as he was away for a long time, I allowed my torpor to take over.

'Miss! Miss!'

'Sally you're wanted out here,' Chico called, and I roused myself quickly so as not to keep the official, now on the boat, waiting and making a bad first impression in Indonesia.

''Ello Miss,' he said affably, as I dropped before him in a manner that could be considered insolent, clad still in my indecorous T-shirt and shorts.

'Hello,' I said, making a phenomenal effort not to sound huffy, whilst at the same time trying not to tower over him in case he had a Napoleon complex. 'Did you want to see me?'

'Yes . . . 'Ello,' he repeated ingenuously, as if unaware he had broken my sleep.

'Hello,' I greeted him again, adding conventionally, without the least wish to know, 'How are you?'

'Well . . . You?'

'Fine!' I replied politely, waking up now and realising he wanted only to have me come at his whim like a soldier to a commanding officer.

'Um, well. Nice to have met you,' I lied, trying to bring our discourse to an end, but the man smiled on – almost leered, in fact – as if content to keep me at attention before him with so many spectators.

I looked at Chico to see if I had done what was expected, and he smiled sympathetically and indicated under raised eyebrows by a flick of his eyes to the cabin interior that I could go back to bed.

It was too late to recapture that delicious drowsiness now, and I stayed on deck to stare back up at the crowds on the passenger ship. Steve was walking along the starboard outrigger keeping *Sari* from pressing too hard against the ship, while shaking hands with lower deck passengers. His intolerance of inexperience was no doubt due to the strain of responsibility at sea, but for the moment he was happy that his maiden voyage as a navigator was over and confidence in his skills seemed to be swelling up. We had survived one stretch of sea with a crew made partly of first-time sailors, a débutant navigator, an untried boat and a load of defective bamboo. The captain had a gammy knee, the first mate a hollow tooth from too much dental flossing, and the cook stomach problems. Things could only get better, couldn't they?

6. Sulawesi slalom

The soldiers in *imigrasi* seemed enamoured of the red tape with which their job was festooned, probably because they were grateful for the break from routine our visit promised. On that first morning, having been surprised to find we had no guns to protect ourselves from pirates, and disconcerted by our amusement at being asked point blank whether we were carrying drugs (as if they expected a spontaneous confession from smugglers), they walked around the boat showing the same disdain for privacy that the Filippinos had. They stared into the cabin at resting crew members, fingering our possessions and even consulting together over the photograph of Steve's girlfriend, which they removed from the bamboo slat of the cabin wall. This was obviously normal in this part of the world, however, and we *were* much more entertaining than the usual visitors.

'Come on, Sal,' Chico called a couple of days later. 'We've got to have our photos taken!'

We entered the immigration building by the quay and, instead of the third degree treatment we had expected to accompany our mugshots, we found we had joined a friendly social gathering where we were offered cold tea (the usual way of drinking it in Indonesia). How I would love to have that photograph of Chico and I together, taken against a bare wall, as we peered wide-eyed with incredulity into the lens, our lips pursed to hold in the guffaws we were suppressing!

'We need fingerprints too,' we were told, and they certainly did – in quadruplicate. This little pantomime was even more testing to our decorous demeanor. Each person had the thumb and each finger of both hands rolled on the ink pad in turn, the guiding officer then making a perfect imprint on official forms with boxes drawn out for each digit.

'It is finish . . . for now,' the chief said eventually as we stood like recently washed-up surgeons, holding our limp-wristed hands away from all contact, waiting our turn to wash them.

'Come back before you leave the town and we will do it again!'

'I think we'll give that a swerve,' Smiley and Steve both muttered under their breath.

In spite of their unforgettable presence in our lives, the immigration men went to great lengths to help us, even posting a guard on the boat so we could all go out together. They escorted us into town in the rain which had spoilt the day of our arrival. By the time we returned, in a *bemo* (a public transport van), the tide had gone out and left *Sari* listing towards a supporting outrigger. The party continued on the slanting bow. As the only female there, the remarks directed at me by the Indonesian men were mostly flippant or flirtatious, which, though harmless, seemed rather condescending and I escaped to bed at the earliest opportunity I could seize without seeming impolite.

The next night I was the wet blanket again when the men went to socialise at the local brothel. Bob came back early in the evening to fetch the guitar and told me how things were going.

'They're all making eyes at Smiley,' he said, puzzling over it. 'You're a woman,' (they had noticed), 'do you find him attractive?'

The family nearest the sea ran a *rumah makan* (small 'eating house') and we became friendly enough to be invited to bathe in their shower room. The quayside was reached at high tide by *sampan* rides, with which the fishermen were very generous. We washed our clothes on the stony shore with little shrimp-like crustacea darting about over the stones at our feet, and it was lovely to ladle fresh water over our heads from the bucket after days of salt-water ablutions. It was also infinitely more hygienic than the sluggish water full of household effluent which raised our anchored boat off the bottom coming in and bumped her down again with each low tide.

Shopping was done every day at the market. José was happy to have such a variety of food. So happy, in fact, that returning from the market with squid, fish, meat, eggs and bean curd, he would cook most of it for one meal without a thought for the morrow. I suppose this is the way of people who are poor, filling up while food is available and starving when it is not. Here among plenty, this glut of good food was not so damaging (though Bob's resources must have been dwindling fast), but at sea, when we could not replenish supplies, José's feast and famine tactics would reduce us, after two days of gourmet delights, to unappetising rice, onions and noodles.

As well as his work, José's social life was mostly separate from that of the rest of the crew. He sometimes went off with his new-found friend, Heinrich, to look for gold and diamonds. He was obsessed with making a fortune, and his tales of adventure in his mysterious past included magnificent finds of ores and precious stones. Learning quickly how to use the town grapevine, he had found a kindred spirit in Heinrich and, though they did not strike it rich, they did find a great deal to talk about, and the thrill of the hunt seemed almost as intoxicating as a find.

One afternoon, I went for a walk in the country and was soon full to overflowing with tea, both hot and cold. Hospitality in the poorer houses seemed to be out of pure interest in a rare foreign visitor, but the richer ones were more concerned with my possessions and status. During my chats, I needed every one of the words I had learnt so far, and tried to guess the meaning of many more. it was not until I returned to the boat that the laughter and disbelief some of my answers had elicited was explained.

'Bob,' I called as soon as I got back, consulting our best speaker of *Bahasa Indonesia*. 'Does *kawin* means the same as *kawan?*' I had made the assumption throughout the afternoon that it was a local pronunciation variation of the word for 'friend'.

'No. Why?' he looked up with the enquiry.

'Well, everyone kept asking me if I had *kawin* and I said that I had six back on the boat,' I replied, waiting for enlightenment.

'That's good,' he laughed with his infectious chesty chuckle. 'It means "marriage"!'

Repair and improvement work began on the sails. Each one was staked out on the sand anchored by coarse grass in front of the warehouse, and we took up our needles like the men sewing up the copra-filled sacks nearby. The sails were too heavy for the yards, and, being mere rectangles, could not belly out to make the best use of the wind. A boat *tukang*, or skilled shipwright, was consulted and he showed Bob how to shape them to resemble the 'crab's claw' sails of the Pacific. Curves were cut into the sides, after which the hemming and bolt-rope sewing had to be repeated.

The bamboo water containers had become filled with toadstools which caused a terrible stench, so they were now split up for use as building material, as were the old outriggers, since the deck was already showing its weakness. Bamboo for more buoyant outriggers was sought and this involved trips into the surrounding area to cut some from the town headman's groves. The journey was like a holiday outing, as most trips with Bob – whether for business or pleasure – turned out to be, so adept had he become at getting the best out of time with these unhurried people. We forded the wide river overlooked by the hillside plantations of olive-green clove trees, and young men cut down the most suitable pieces from a thicket.

Afterwards Bob visited the *dukun* or traditional healer whom a new friend had recommended to treat his knee. We entered the wooden hut and the *dukun* brought out an ointment and some of the same leaves the traditional healer near Manila had used, massaging the knee in a way that impressed Bob with its efficacy.

'This man's good,' he murmured as we watched him push the swollen flesh away from the knee, above and below, as if trying to disperse the fluid.

'How can you tell?' asked Chico.

'Because it hurts like hell!' he gasped.

The joint did feel looser afterwards and I tried to continue the massage during the rest of the voyage, discovering that strength as well as skill is needed as the intensely muscular work began to make my hands ache. The massage parlour minutes were oases of tranquillity at the end of each day when I was sometimes taken into Chico and Bob's collective confidence. We discussed the 'three boys'. Smiley had not excelled in enterprise or dynamism, and had spent almost his entire time, when not on watch, sleeping on whichever bunk was free. It was clear that Bob would get rid of him when we got to Bali, and I felt quite sorry since he was far from being an antagonistic or disruptive influence on the crew. He did at least do all that was asked of him but he too had difficulty in sifting out the commands from the chaff of Bob's curiously detailed sentences and was also verbally lambasted for not 'taking the initiative'.

Talk of fundamental changes in Bali caused me to worry again about my own position, but my hard work seemed to be recognised now that I had set to the tasks of reshaping the sails and redecking parts of the boat with diligence.

We were taken for the day up to the clove plantation. *Cengkeh* (pronounced 'chengkay'), imported originally from Zanzibar and Pemba, have allowed some people to prosper in this part of Sulawesi. At the plantation we discovered there was a transmigrant settlement two hours' walk away.

Java and Bali are overcrowded islands in a nation of enormous reserves of uninhabited land. The government therefore transports, and provides with food and seeds for the first few months, volunteer migrants who choose to leave their cramped island for another where they pioneer a new living. The transmigrants here were some thousand Balinese.

At first I thought the transmigrants were coerced and I felt indignant, but even after finding this was not so, I was not any more enchanted by the policy. Large areas of primary forest are cleared to provide the farming land for these people, and, even after several years of experience and the example of similar Amazonian projects, the lesson that rainforest soil fertility is maintained only by the continued existence of the forest upon it does not seem to have been learnt. After one or two growing seasons the land ends up stripped of all its nutrients, as they have been taken up by the plants removed for human consumption and not returned when the plants die, and the cycle of growth is broken. Erosion of the unanchored earth and the necessity for the transmigrants to cut down another temporarily fertile area are accelerating the commercial timber companies' destruction of the forests. Is this a preferable alternative to population control of the most crowded islands, whose ethnic people by transmigration also threaten to swamp the smaller tribes and bring a stultifying uniformity to the nation in the process?

I broached the subject of a visit to the settlement, but Steve told me roughly that we did not have time as we had so much work to do on the boat. He was quite nasty with me these days and I suffered unjust reproofs from him almost as often as I had done from Bob in Languyan. Bob's apparent new respect for my dedication to the success of the expedition meant he was much better to be with, and along with Chico we had some pleasant times. Chico was more relaxed since our departure from his imprisoning island and he began to take time off to go to the market or elsewhere to draw.

He was so taken with the face of the *patrona* in a restaurant that he drew her portrait in pencil on the edge of the white table top, while the children looking over his shoulder reported in muted voices on every pencil stroke – a practice which would normally harass him out of his concentration.

After a week of alterations the boat was ready for a sea trial with the new outriggers and reshaped sails. They were a success, and *Sari* could now sail further to windward. We had just turned happily back towards the shore when the *tukang*'s straw hat was blown off. Urged roguishly by Bob to get it for him, I hesitated a moment, then decided it was a nice enough day for a swim and dived off the deck.

Bob had not really been serious and kept his eyes forward. With a frisson of fear, I saw the boat sailing on without me, conscious that this was only a fraction of the horror that such an abandonment would cause in the open sea, especially if someone fell off unseen at night.

'Hey! Sally's in the water!' Chico cried, a few seconds later, relieving my fear, but the panic rose again as they mocked, 'See you back on shore, Sal!' and turned their backs as if to sail home without me. I tired quickly in the water and could not have made it back to the anchorage, but luckily they were jesting and soon slowed to let me catch up and reboard by walking up an outrigger arm.

The boat was pulled up on shore for cleaning, caulking and anti-fouling treatment and then, ten days after arriving, we were ready to depart. I was nervous the night before leaving, expecting to be blundering about in the pre-dawn darkness, still not having learnt that 'early start' means 'sometime before nightfall'. In the late afternoon, when we finally got underway, the *tukangs* sailed some way out with us, and reassured us that the outriggers were supposed to ride under the water at the stern. When they had left for shore on a *sampan* and we were alone again, sails were put up with the wind and taken down without problems. During a lull in the wind, a third piece of bamboo was added to an outrigger, bound on tightly with rattan. Chico took the opportunity of our light duties and the excuse of Don's birthday to dress as Neptune – a little early, since this ceremony is usually reserved for the crossing of the equator.

'Sally . . . Sally . . . Sally!'

The irritating noise would not go away.

'Come on, it's your watch,' Chico whispered hoarsely through the bunk side window.

'Oh, it can't be yet,' I groaned to myself as I creaked to a sitting position. Having put on more clothes and shambled to the helm, I snuggled down into the cockpit hole for fear of falling asleep and over the side. My watch was now with Steve from four to eight, the time he always kept so he could do dawn and dusk fixes of our position. It was harder to get up at 4am for this shift after broken nights than it was to rise 'normally' at eight, but, as Steve had said to kindle my enthusiasm for it at the start, 'It's the best watch. You see the sunrise every day.'

The sunsets were beautiful, as was the slow transformation of the grey serge sky to a diamond-studded black velvet. Sunrises were even lovelier, and the gold and pink on the horizon was more appreciated, vitiated as it was by small clouds, greyed by the brightness of the halo the low sun behind cast around them.

The water remained calm, though the wind was propelling us rapidly along the coast. When the sails alone were used, we seemed to skim over the water and, with the extended deck, seemed in danger of taking flight. Looking at the steering oar parting the waters before it, our speed was apparent and made me tingle with excitement. In overcast weather the dark water hid everything below the iron-grey surface and my imagination could range freely over the number and diversity of creatures that might be below.

In the sunlight, the hull and outriggers left a glittering wake, which at night sparkled silver and green with the luminescence of tiny creatures. The water seemed almost weightless and it always came as a surprise, when the tiller had to be moved, how heavy and powerful it actually was.

Wednesday, 23rd May

Up for a while during the night to put up the sails and take them down again. We put the sails up later, but couldn't get into the village that we wanted to because both wind and swell were against us. We set off instead for Palu, but then the mainsail boom broke. Although the shrouds have been tightened on the mast, the mast stay on the port side is still pulling out of the base with the force of the wind, and we have had to use the mizzen.

I helped Bob move the bamboos for a new boom, and one of the reshaped sails was put up. It's very difficult to steer the course we want, and the sail keeps luffing (becoming ruffled by the wind at the leading, or luff, edge). Chico nearly capsized us today, trying to sail too close to the wind. In the end, the wind was right on the starboard beam and we stopped moving forward, the weight of the wind gathered in the sail with no spill-off, and began to push the mast down. Since the mast is fixed into the hull, the whole boat began to tip over. Don noticed first, shouting a warning and scrambling over to the starboard outrigger. We all looked up, saw the port outrigger was already deep under the water and made a dash to join him, lunging for the furthest part of the deck, or even for the outrigger, like people diving for cover. Luckily our weight forced the boat upright again while the lower (leach) sheet was loosened and Chico put the wind a little behind the beam. This never happens when the sail is on the starboard. Perhaps there is less weight there.

'How will we know when we're crossing the equator?' I asked around midday.

'We already did about half an hour ago. Didn't you see the line floating on the sea?' Steve quipped.

'Ha, bloody ha. But really, we ought to celebrate. We'll only be doing it once,' I said, naïvely.

In the afternoon we had to turn north-westward to avoid getting too close to shore and being driven on to the rocks, and we crossed the divide again.

Thursday, 24th May
I kept waking up last night and noticed at 3.30am that everyone was in bed except Smiley and that we were drifting. The swells breaking against the hull were making such a noise that I thought we were still moving. I got up and watched until light. Cool. Nice to be alone, but a little worrying because I kept thinking I could see lights.

Today, Bob and Steve have been planning how to get away with the wind against us. Eventually we put up the sail and used the engines as well. (Steve repaired it again yesterday.) We had to dive in and swim the boat round to the right direction again. Soon we'll be crossing the equator for the fifth time!

Friday, 25th May

I woke at 1am to find everyone except José and me on deck, trying to find a way into the port in Donggala. I decided to get up and help them worry, since I wasn't much use for anything else just then.

We had difficulty getting in, but eventually tied up to the *ASEAN Damai*. First thing this morning, Bob, Chico and Steve went off to see the port authorities. While they were away, the tide changed and we were pushed into the lee of the *ASEAN* and had to push off her with poles. The problem was temporarily solved by tying on to her by the stern and untying the bowline, after which we were pushed against her other side where we retied the bow. We fought to the point of exhaustion against being pushed broadside on to her on one side or the other, until the complete change of tide kept us at a safe distance. I'm now thoroughly depressed at my own incompetence and our helplessness against the elements.

This afternoon we moved into shallower water. Bob has already found a ship *tukang* to adjust the masts. He helped us into the harbour where Bob made further enquiries about the tide and snapped at Don, whose *Bahasa Indonesia* is rapidly becoming very good, when he did the same.

José and I went to the market this afternoon, then met up with Steve and Smiley in the bar. I saw a large hawk catch a fish with its claws in the sea.

Saturday, 26th May

Everyone went to bed early just when I didn't feel like it, for a change! José and I went to the market again. When we got back to the harbour, the tide was very low, so we just walked out through the dirty water. There were some motionless brown things on the bottom which turned out to be small fish that swam off when we came close. I wonder why they all stay motionless like that. Sunbathing?

In the afternoon I walked out along the road to Kilo Tiga (Kilometre Three) – not a very inspiring name for a village. There were some lovely scenes along the way, with bullock carts and houses with flowers in the garden, but I escaped on a lorry back to Donggala when a whole schoolful of kids poured out of the playground to follow me.

Sandeqs or *sundeys* (small double-outrigger sailing boats) dot the harbour mouth like white swans between the blue sky and bluer sea. This evening we ate under an awning made of a sail, listening to 'Voice of America' on the radio, feeling like wealthy cruisers at Cannes among all the other spruce yachts.

I did not enjoy the shopping in the next few days because José insisted on coming along even though it was not necessary. I suppose, like me, he needed an excuse for an outing, but would not go alone. I think he was discomfited because people took him to be an Indonesian, plaguing him with attempts at conversation he could not understand, and he feared to make a terrible *faux pas* which would not be excused so easily of him as it would be of me.

Back at the boat I tried to learn his culinary skills. I might have been tempted to learn from the carpenters, too, as they chipped away at the boat, but their skIll was so consummate and their confidence so profound that they swung axes high and buried them in wood between closely placed bare feet without fear for their toes, and tapped chisels crotch-ward with such lack of concern for their manhood that I dared not look.

The Chinese family on the shore now showed us hospitality, and Santi, the daughter, found the association with our expedition a thrilling source of gossip at school. There was a holiday on the first day of Ramadan which Santi, as a non-Muslim with no need to fast during the day, could enjoy. She invited me to the swimming baths a few miles away on the back of her small Japanese motorbike. She was quite proficient on it, but I soon felt that black leather gear with studs and a skull and crossbone painted on the jacket would have been more appropriate than her feminine summer clothes. We chased down the road at full throttle in a cloud of dust, seemingly oblivious of the dangers of the road, overtaking on bend and hill and nipping smartly back on to our side of the road when a lorry appeared suddenly round or over it.

I realised that bikinis would not be approved of in this Muslim society, and had brought my one-piece bathing costume, but soon found that even with this I had underestimated the prudishness of society. Eventually I stepped coyly out of the cubicle and plunged into the murky water of the swimming pool in my everyday sea wear of T-shirt (with bra underneath, of course) and shorts. Thinking out small talk in *Bahasa Indonesia* up to your neck in tepid, cloudy tea is trying, and we exhausted all topics of conversation in no time. Yet, apart from the fully dressed bathers and the unsolicited mudpack, it was a curiously familiar scene, complete with poolside Coke drinkers and hand-holding lovers.

Friday, 1st June

I was woken at 4am by the muezzins' call to prayer from the various mosques within earshot. The tide was still coming in and I felt the boat right itself as it was lifted off the sand. We have had a few miscalculations of tides and false starts, but this time we managed to get seaborne again. The backstay beams of the mast now straddle the width of the deck with a block of wood aligning the three pieces of wood at the summit. The holes in the roof of the cabin where the backstays used to pass through have been rather ineffectively repaired by rearrangement of the nipa, so now it's preferable to sleep with the feet at that end of the bunk. The cabin is becoming very rickety. It's being eaten away by a small species of beetle which is proliferating in the bamboo. The dust their excavations produce powders us like snow and fills the cabin with clouds whenever something is moved – not very good for cameras and the sextant.

The mizzen mast has been cut down, simplifying matters, but when we raised the sail on the main (which should perhaps now be referred to as 'The Only') at about 8am, a large rip in it became apparent, along with a number of small holes that make it look like a moth-eaten curtain. It's unfortunate we didn't see the damage when we had terra firma on which to stretch it out for mending, but we've been doing our best to sew on patches on small exposed areas, re-rolling them afterwards and unravelling another part to work on. As I helped Chico to apply the patches, we chattered of commonplace things as if at a suburban sewing circle making appliqué bedspreads, though perched on the narrow bow deck, with our feet dangling over the lovely blue water, rushing backwards and glittering in the sun, the link with suburbia was tenuous.

When the sail was flown at last, patched with new white circles, squares and ovals on the greenish grey of the moulding canvas, the wind sped us along the coast at four knots for a few hours before it died and then changed direction.

Saturday, 2nd June

My four to eight watch was OK, although it was windy, with showers. Some of the other watches got soaked, though. We put things out to dry and continued motoring. We came across more *sundeys*, from which we obtained some lovely fish in exchange for a little flour. (I find that although we still approach other boats cautiously, I no longer expect to meet pirates. Perhaps we don't look affluent enough to be worth attacking.)

José worked wonders with the fish and even made a cake in the afternoon, but his elaborate meals leave him too tired to help with other tasks. I tried to persuade him to save his energy for a marathon, rather than using it all up in these stunning sprints, but it's no good. After cooking, he just lies like the dead on his short mat under Bob's bunk and can do nothing for the rest of the day.

Sunday, 3rd June

We approached Mamuju at 4.30am, but even then there were enough people in flowing robes returning from the mosque to make up an audience, without which we would now feel almost incomplete. I walked along the outrigger to stop it bumping and fell in, wearing my only warm clothes, the track suit Bob had lent me.

'Sally's in again! She must like getting wet!' Steve joshed.

'Ah, a volunteer!' Bob cried joyfully. 'Since you're already in, be a love and swim the bowline over to the quay,' he pleaded, and I walked on the bottom in the heavy clothes and handed it up to a bewildered onlooker who secured it for us.

Our breakfast of fish, rice, papaya and biscuits was enjoyed by all who watched. Cheers went up from shore whenever a head popped out of the hatches, and Bob's compulsory trip to the authorities looked like a subdued carnival procession. We moved later to a jetty made of a long stone walk ending with a crossbar of concrete and wood, in the vain hope that it would be more secluded.

This is a lovely-looking place, with lush green hills rising behind the town and giving it the feeling of a warm Scotland with mosques. I wandered off alone to the edge of town where I discovered people much less oppressive in their interest in us, and spied over a hedge that sure mark of 'civilisation': a tennis court. On my return, the stone pier hosted a crowd of children and men staring at the boat in the hope of seeing the slightest movement of the occupants, but there was none, and I sat among the mooners being questioned and scrutinised until the napping inmates saw me and Chico came to ferry me home.

Steve and Smiley went into town this evening. The wind and tide changed while they were away and, when I realised there was something wrong, I went out in the rain and saw that the boat was being pushed against the pier. After trying unsuccessfully to motor out, we walked down an outrigger to push *Sari* off. This didn't work either, so I was ordered to climb up the wooden scaffolding on to the pier, which seemed already as high out of the water as a cliff. I was supposed to tie the end of a rope to the capstan-like post on top, but it was too short to reach.

I rushed around calling for further instructions. Chico and Don were being crushed against the pier, balanced on the slippery outriggers, shoulders pressed to the scaffold, groaning and sweating with the toil while José pushed with his small body against the structure with a bamboo pole from his place on deck. The *pamalongs* also had to be saved from a nose-or tail-on confrontation with anything solid since the force could allow the curved planks, held in the timber at front and back, to spring out and open up bow or stern.

At Bob's instigation, I threw down a coiled rope, only to be damned for not retaining one end of it. The end of the rope from which I had untied the knot wriggled over the ground like a fugitive snake as I, recovering from the confusion, realised I needed it. It receded only feet from me, squirming in the poor light, always just out of reach until it plunged off the precipice to the sea below. My lunges for it nearly dealt me a similar fate. It was terrifying on that high platform, running to catch ropes and carry out instructions in the dim light filtering up from the boat, without my glasses and with the invisible edge such a danger. It was like the chase at the climax of a thriller, over skyscraper roofs but without the city lights or the circumference wall to check a fall. I ran about trying to help, crossing and recrossing the foot-wide gap in the jetty through which I could see the water heaving and swirling around the pillars far below.

Those on the boat finally managed to motor out and return on the lee of the jetty. Chico tried to throw up a line for me to secure, but it was too high and the rope end splashed back into the sea as he was called away, confused and abused by Bob. This time he answered back. I could hear him in the distance, as the rain's hiss grew quieter, complaining of Bob's unclear instructions, while Don swam over with the line and climbed part way up the scaffold to pass it to me.

Panic over, I climbed down to get the rubber ducky from the windward side of the pier, but the current was too strong for me to paddle round, and the legs of the pier were too far apart for me to pull the boat along by hand. After a few tries, I gave up and climbed the scaffold again. Surprisingly, our struggles drew few spectators, and no one came to help. As I climbed back, one man was watching from the edge of the pier, so bewildered by this sort of behaviour in a woman that he just remained squatting there when I met him head-on. I had to ask him to move so I could climb on to the platform.

I strolled the dark way along the top, stepping over the gap and noticing how wide it seemed now that I was not jumping it at a run. I slowed when I thought the other end must be near, climbed down carefully, startling and being startled by the crabs disturbed from the wooden beams of the framework, and swam the few yards back to the boat. When Steve and Smiley returned, they called to us.

'That looked like fun.'

'We saw it from the bar, but we didn't think we could help.'

'Well, you can help now. Bring the ducky around, will you?' Bob asked, and they did with no trouble at all, because, I consoled myself, the current is not so strong now.

Monday, 4th June

The spectators soon returned once the rain had stopped and one tried to negotiate the sale of a white cockateel from the top of the jetty. I turned away to sleep, leaving Bob to it. I was pleased, when I got up for my watch at 3am, to find no bird on board and no one watching from the jetty. I was only supposed to do an hour, to stop any further suicide attempts by *Sari*, but it was so pleasant in the calm, lonely night, that I stayed up until dawn, reading *Mutiny On The Bounty* by lamplight.

The muezzin called and there was a sermon over a loudspeaker at about four, and the little boys collected on the jetty to shout, ''Ello Misterrrr!' at five.

Although further repairs are still needed, we can't bear as much attention as we have been getting. The changing tides were also causing great difficulties, so we left Mamuju without regrets this morning. A short sail down the coast brought us to a beautiful bay where gleaming white *sundeys* with fine blue-striped sails dart over the water or are beached on the gently sloping shore.

'Look at that, Sal!' Bob said, his voice swooping up on my shortened name. 'Much better than Mamuju, eh?' and we headed in happily for a closer look at this jewel of white sand pressed to the sea by the jade hills beyond.

We did not even attempt to pin *Sari* to this fine sand, though Bob has acquired a metal anchor which is obviously much more effective than the 'neolithic' wooden one made by The Boys. We tied to a large wooden barge loaded with cattle and buffalo. Later we had yet another pitched battle with the high wind, using all our available ropes to tie to a palm tree on the distant shore.

The barge's crew came over and coveted everything we have. On our return visit this evening we did the same, finding the arrangement of men and cattle in their boat quite comfortable, though the vessel, a junk-shaped barge, is so low in the water that the slightest ripple could send water over the gunwale. Obviously this is what they are used to since the sides above that are completely closed over – a kind of oversealing which makes us quite envious of their dry, but cramped bunks below, warmed by the presence of the cattle, even if they are smelly – though they still have to take care not to be swamped by larger waves. They have been waiting for two days for calmer conditions so that the overloaded vessel can cross to Borneo to pick up timber and return with equal disregard for the Plimsoll line. With squalls and storms so unpredictable, they are taking a diabolical personal risk.

There's bamboo in a nearby village and Bob will go for it tomorrow. I'm looking forward to a walk in this beautiful village.

The *sampans* here had no outriggers and the slightest fidgeting inside their narrow hull could tip them over. I got a lift in one, sitting like a statue, over to the nearest beach of Labu Labuan, and walked north along the coast road to the market in Somba. José didn't come, but of course I was not alone. My initially large entourage of children grew, each child encountered on the way clinging like iron filings to a magnet, until, by the time I reached the market square, there was a crowd of a hundred or more trailing behind me. Their chattering excitement rose to a crescendo of screams of laughter at anything I did, such as sneeze, which was so remarkably identical to the way they did it.

I went early every day to the market, passing emerald green paddy fields scarred by clearings where coffee was grown. I never evaded the crowds of children who swarmed like worker bees around the queen and had to part the Red Sea of bodies whenever I wanted to see the fruit and vegetables displayed on the ground. I was pleased to be far from tourist areas, but missed the comparative anonymity such places lend.

The beach was too shallow at Labu Labuan to bring the boat on shore so she was sailed half a mile north to Somba where the slope was steeper and she could be brought in close enough to be left high and dry twice a day. We were easier to watch from here, however, and a crowd like that in an amphitheatre stood on the short, steep slope throughout the day in two 'sittings', as the schoolchildren, who go to school only in the morning or the afternoon, handed over shifts.

Bob moved swiftly to speed our getaway. He had to acquire yet more new outriggers since the others had not been good enough for a long journey. The best bamboo that could be found was especially large *katigs* from *sundeys*. These were painted, however, and we had to start by scraping off the white paint with knives.

This, too, was a fascinating spectator sport, and we worked between hedges three-deep of children which increased in thickness when we emerged from between the houses to scrape the part of the outrigger lying on the spacious beach. The privileged front line stood so close that the white powder we blew off our patch of work got into their eyes, but instead of moving further away, they blinked hard and looked accusingly at us as if we should stop what we were doing to accommodate them.

The sails were also reshaped and sewn, and in the evenings we nursed blistered thumbs, cramped hands and bad backs. Having once taken the initiative of lighting the lamps in Languyan, the responsibility for this task had since become mine. I now lit the lamps each night wherever we were. It was especially difficult at sea trying to get the kerosene into the plastic funnel as we rocked and jolted over the swells. After a hard day at this work I lay flat on the hard bunk to relieve my back, hoping someone else would take the trouble for a change. They did eventually, when it was too dark for the descent of night to be ignored any longer, but I felt guilty not continuing a task which, solely by habit, had become my duty. My aching hands did not make a very good job of the daily massage of Bob's knee.

'You know, I'm glad you're here with us,' Chico told me, making me glow as I worked away at the leg. 'You take the trouble and have compassion for everyone,' he said again, as he had said at sea when I dispensed drinks or did little fiddly jobs without protest. He still did not discern my special interest in him, though I felt it must be obvious to everyone else.

His presence at any gathering made the simplest occasions fun. He seemed to like being with me too, but he liked women generally and to him I was just the 'girl next door'. Now that my back was painful, he massaged it, and the sensation was a temptation like that of the smell of a lovely meal to a gourmet not allowed to eat. I was fed up of my wholesome, sexless image and knew if I got the chance I would not squander another night alone with him on qualms about morality.

7. A brush with Borneo

Bathing was done either very publicly at the washing well which was green with moss and resembled a fairy grotto inside, or more privately in the sea where we dived and barked like seals. Drinking water was collected from a pump where I found one particular admirer insistent on pumping up our enormous requirements for the next part of the voyage, smiling coyly as each jerry can was handed over.

He would have carted it to the boat as well but I drew the line there and, having passed all the cans up to the men, I negotiated the hanging rope to climb on to the boat at the high bow, failing and falling often to the evident gratification of the crowd. When the amphitheatre was especially full, Chico entertained the children with his clowning, which was, of course, a mistake, but the urge to do something outrageous was so strong before that expectant sea of faces.

The wooden houses actually on the beach were on stilts. The alleys between them presented a perfect portrait of the fisherman's life. I was especially interested to find boats in construction, from *sampans* to large boats higher than the houses, which I doubted could be brought down to the sea without the demolition of a hut. Some bristled all over the hull with protruding wooden pegs, like hedgehogs stranded on their backs. Traditional methods were still employed and there were few modern tools, so the interest in our own craft was strong.

The tide changes for which Somba beach had been chosen were a hazard. Waves came in and receded with such force that little boys body-surfed on the small rollers, but, at a certain tide level, the waves which dumped on to the sand raised the *Sarimanok* up and let her down with such a thud on the shore that she twisted with the impact. There was a grave danger that the force would cause the planks to spring out from their pinions at the bow and stern *pamalongs*.

We lashed on the newly scraped outrigger bamboos with rattan, tightening it mercilessly with the leverage of a wooden shuttle-like device which we had been lent and hammering the weave with a mallet. The deck was repaired also, which meant days of broiling heat, alternating with sea dips if the rain did not come to cool us.

Tuesday 12th to Thursday 14th June

I felt rather hard-done-by all Tuesday morning as I repaired the decking while Steve and Smiley swam and read. I was also feeling grumpy since José told me I'm getting fat. I keep trying to eat less, but I was disgusted at what a mess I look when I saw myself in a mirror for the first time in weeks on that day out from Donggala.

Don got back from looking for a place to change money (he had to go as far as Pare Pare) in the afternoon, so we left in the evening. There was no wind at first, but when it came rushing up from behind, we sped along at five knots. We were just congratulating ourselves on the perfect heading we were making when the steering oar broke in two. We could see it bending under the water as Steve had great difficulty holding it steady before it broke. Luckily (or, rather, owing to good forethought) Bob had made a hole at the base of the blade, through which a thin rope was threaded to secure it to the rig. We lowered the sail quickly, pulled in the broken part of the oar, unlashed the shaft from the post and the boat skidded sideways with no steerage.

Putting in the other, very heavy, steering oar was difficult and dangerous. Nearly everyone had to help because of the weight, but we couldn't all congregate around the post. Then the water was already pulling it out of our hands as it was being lashed in place. We tried to sail again by setting the mizzen sail on the 'Only' mast, hoping that we would slow down, but, within minutes, the second oar broke even more violently than the first.

With no rudder or keel, the boat slid over the surface as its structure dictated, and this decreed that the swells should be taken beam-on. The large approaching wave raised up one outrigger, tipping the boat alarmingly, passed under the hull then raised the other one, threatening to topple the boat the other way just as another surge made its attack on the first side. The motion of the boat was not only violent and extreme enough to make us feel sick, it also petrified us with fear that the next swell would be just a little higher and turn the boat right over.

We tried everything to make *Sari* take the swells head-on and stop this dangerous and uncomfortable tantrum. After dark the smallest storm-sail was stretched between the mast and one back-stay, all hands holding it there by force as the wind blew into it to swing the bow around. We had some success, but once the alignment was right, we could hold it only briefly before she swung around further to place us side-on to the seas again.

The very thick rope now found a use. It was dragged up from the hold with great effort, tied by one end to the rear *pamalong* and the rest of the coiled bundle was dropped overboard in the hope that its weight would take it down to the deeper, relatively still water and that the current would trail the boat out from this 'anchor' and face the stern into the flow. All these devices, tried repeatedly with small variations learnt by experience, only exhausted us.

A steering oar was mended as well as possible, but it was not strong enough to stand up to the boat being driven by sail or motor. While it stopped our skimming over the surface, it did not reduce the exaggerated motion.

I didn't get to bed until after my watch, at 4am, spent anxiously looking out to make sure the lighthouse did not come any nearer. The boat's motion made it feel as if we were on an interminable funfair ride. It became quite exciting once I realised that *Sari* probably wouldn't fall to bits, but I was heartily sick of it by the time the rain came to calm the sea, around midday. It makes everything so difficult. Even going along the deck to fetch a cup from the roof guttering is a major expedition, with rest stops along the way. Steve is always telling me to keep one hand for myself and one for the boat – in other words to hang on to something fixed to the boat – but the cabin is no longer fixed down very well thanks to the burrowing of the beetles. I keep expecting the whole thing, swaying and creaking like a fat woman's stays, to come away in my hand and dump me helpless, but not strictly homeless, over the side.

Going to the loo, which is usually done at the end of an outrigger arm, is now often done with difficulty from the edge of the deck. I envy the boys their convenient 'pee shooters'. When the seas died a little yesterday, we returned to the outrigger arms where the paired S-connectors are beautifully spaced to be used like a toilet seat.

'Hey! Its like going in a washing machine!' Steve called back from his comfortable dunny seat.

'No need for loo paper either, it cleans you up at the same time!'

When I got up from a short sleep after the night watch, the others were already up and making a rudder out of bamboo slats, like the construction of the decking. The theory was that, with the spaces allowing some of the water through, it shouldn't break so easily, but when we tried it, it wasn't effective either. Chico did most of the steering on our watch, trying to keep the swells on the port quarter, but it's really difficult with the wind coming from a different direction. We had to pump the bilge at the end of the watch, so we didn't get to bed until 4.45am.

We were up again at around 7.30am today and did not stop working all day. The sail ripped in the morning, and Bob and I sewed it. It ripped again in the afternoon, and I actually volunteered to mend it, so that I wouldn't be called upon to do it outside my watch. In the end, it took me a lot longer anyway.

José is feeling seasick and we had no lunch. He says it's his stomach ulcer bothering him, probably due to the tense situation, and he hardly eats anything. Bob cooked supper and asked José to sew, but he wasn't even up to doing that, so I did some more.

We continued like convicts stitching mail bags until Don wanted the large sail moved forward so he could reach the end hanging over the sea at the stern, wrapped around the yard and boom.

'Right now!' he added when I delayed for a second to secure the needle in the cloth, and I rushed to grab the bundle with both hands, since it is too heavy to inch along with one. As I did so, the vindictive *Sari* tipped suddenly to starboard and flipped me head over heels into the water. As I surfaced through a fizzing cloud of froth, I could see the bare soles of a worried-looking Chico as the slats of the deck moved over me. Illogically, I reached up to grasp it, although I knew it was too high. As soon as I realised that that was no good, I pushed off with a foot from the hull to reach the outrigger just in time to catch the last of the four pairs of S-connectors as it glided over the sea.

'Keep your mouth closed,' Don advised as I gasped for breath to haul myself back on board and took in mouthfuls of sea water instead.

'I've got to breathe!' I complained indignantly, taking in more water. He walked along a strong *batangan* beam and crouched with outstretched hand to help me up, smiling sympathetically, rather than appearing to make fun of me. The others were nice about it too, although they dared not come to help for fear of tipping the boat over.

I feel a fool. Everyone says I should have held on to something, but it was impossible to move the booms at the same time. Bob is sure I won't fall in again. No one ever does after the shock of it, he says, but it's not so easy as all that. I go around on all fours now to reach the helm, since there is nothing to hold on to on the narrow stern deck, but I am exasperated by the laughter I then get from the very people who advise me to take such precautions. If any of us falls in, it will be the nightmare slow death I envisaged when I jumped into the sea for the *tukang*'s hat. Bob said he will put a rope on the *pamalong* at the stern to trail out behind. Theoretically, if anyone does fall overboard, they have a chance to catch hold of that. He hasn't done anything about it yet, and I don't really think anything will come of it.

Smiley kindly finished the sewing for me.

Friday, 15th June
I got wet again last night! I was woken by a couple of gallons of water which sloshed up from the sea and came through the cabin wall as if it wasn't there. I changed clothes, but now have no dry ones left, so took great care when we had to go out to take the sail down. I 'slept' in the middle of the cabin between the two bunk shelves, because bunk and bedding are wet. Chico and I are now on the dreaded four to eight watch. He climbs the mast several times each day to hammer in the block of wood which is bound to the three poles as, chafing with the motion of the deck, they regularly eject it.

Apart from the dreadful hours, watches are much better with Chico. He takes a good turn at the helm while we compete to

guess what time it is before I check with the clock over his bed.
He even allowed me to sleep on one afternoon when there were no
other duties, but I felt compelled to come out to relieve him when I
looked up to see him vainly trying to roll a cigarette with one hand,
unable to release the jolting tiller. When sailing and motoring are
impossible, we sit out together in the lee of the cabin, helping to
hold it up, stare out to sea and chat, though the conversation is
never deep, with all the fears we have to distract us.

After overstaying my watch in the night, I slept soundly until
woken by Bob. The usual imperative tone of his voice roused me
immediately with misgivings that I was to make the breakfast or be
hauled up for some other task.

'Cocoa?' he offered.

'Oh! Er, yes please!' I said, unable to hide my surprise.

'You should have seen your face,' he jibed. 'You thought I was
going to get you to cook, didn't you?'

'Well, yes,' I admitted, and simpered with humility for having
jumped to the worst, though most likely, conclusion.

Bob's spells in the galley whenever José is ill have already
resulted in a good clearout of the hold where he discovered lots
of goodies squirrelled away. This hoarding of some things seems
out of keeping with José's feckless use of others, but I suppose
it must be worrying when anyone can plunge a hand into the
stores for their own use, then blame the cook when everything
runs out.

Bob was very friendly this evening as I peeled garlic for his
cooking. With Chico looking on, he asked if I would like to come
back next year to complete the voyage to Madagascar, if we don't
make it to Bali in time to catch the trade winds this year before
they become too fierce. I am surprised after all our disagreements,
but really pleased!

Saturday, 16th June

There were no problems on our night watch when we were sailing
with the mizzen. Breakfast was around 10am. With little to do
during the day watch except steer, Chico and I took it in turns and
had a good rest in between.

Steve damaged the sextant yesterday when it fell, so he doesn't
feel he can rely on it now.

above: The house in
Languyan
left: Hull of the
Sarimanok on the
author's arrival in
Languyan
right: Chico measuring
the thickness of the hull
with wooden callipers

previous page top: Chico, Steve and Bob receiving directions to Toli Toli from an Indonesian fisherman near Sulawesi
previous page bottom: Pulling the *Sarimanok* onto the beach, Bali
right: View from the main mast ladder – Steve on helm, with Bob
below: Making palm weave sails in the whaling village of Lamalera

previous page top: Bob rolled up against the storm
previous page bottom: The *Sarimanok* at the Cocos (Keeling) Islands
above: *Pledang* sailing
below: Robin in bow, Don collecting grated coconut on a wooden plate

previous page top left:
Storm sail
previous page top right:
Bob and the author in the
galley
previous page bottom:
Water covering
outriggers and deck
above: Robin and Steve
below: Fishermen pulling
a *jukung* onto the beach,
Bali

above: José and the deck
seen from the main mast
ladder
right: The *Sarimanok* in
Mayotte

'Oh well, I always wanted to go to Sumatra,' he said, after the midday fix yesterday.

'Don't say that. Let's hope we come within reach of Borneo first, we may not have enough water to go that far,' Bob put in, to cheer us up.

We are now in sight of the southern end of Kalimantan (the Indonesian part of Borneo). It came into view soon after Steve told us that we have spent the morning sailing through a mined area! It will still be difficult to reach, though, and we could be swept past.

Sunday, 17th June

We wallowed all night and took short watches. Rain again. We put up the mizzen sail but the boom broke. We prepared another by lashing lengthwise-split pieces of bamboo on either side. We have moved the motor support frame to the port side where we hope the motor will not be swamped so often, so it should be easier to steer west. The casing of the machine is virtually watertight, but the gurgling it makes as it struggles over the swells is heartrending, like someone coming up for their last breath.

We were towed the last part of the way to the tiny island where we are anchored. It's near Pulau Laut ('Sea Island'), off the south-east tip of Borneo. As we approached, we saw the idle sailing boats drawn up neatly on the beach and nestled on slings with smart rope bindings. Their hulls are gleaming white as if newly painted and the red or green lines around the hull are pristine. A launch towed us as high up the shallow sloping beach as possible and in late afternoon I waded the rest of the way ashore.

The whole island shore can be covered on foot in an hour of easy walking. There's no market but the island seems quite prosperous. I waded back wondering what was so enchanting about this place. I think it's because there are no dogs to rush out and harry you when you pass the owner's house, and the animals that are kept are held in neat small pens, some raised off the ground on stilts like the houses beside them. The whole impression of the place is of cleanliness and friendliness.

Returning to the boat, the beauty of the scene was breathtaking. The shallow water was so clear that *Sari*'s shadow was clearly visible below her surrounded by sapphire blue sea, while the sand on the islet behind was snowy white and its coconut palm fronds tickled the milky wisps of cloud in the sky like dusters of dark green feathers. The brightly lit night left us stranded on a desert of dry sand, and Bob and Chico burst upon the scene after a walk on the island overwhelmed by the grace of the *Sarimanok*, silvered by the moon, resting with wings outstretched on her bed of sand.

'She looks like a huge bird on the wastes of Antarctica!' Bob whispered hoarsely, when their crunching tread over the salt-encrusted sand stopped below me. He was right. Their approach left the only two tracks in the vast expanse of white and, if it had not been so warm, I could have sworn there were husky dogs and sledges following them over.

Up early to consider *Sari*'s position with an eye on the purple-black clouds on the horizon, Bob ordered a move further inshore once the tide was high enough, but, soon after taking her place among smaller neighbours facing up the beach, she tried to destroy both them and herself. Or at least that is how it seemed when the sudden squall brought on the biggest threat to her survival yet. The sky darkened with heavy rain clouds until it was blacker than the lovely moonlit night we had just enjoyed. The wind threw the heavy rain down almost horizontally, trying to flatten the slanting palms to the ground. Some of their deep green 'feathers', tossing about like hydra tentacles, were plucked from the crown, crashing to the ground only feet away from the sheltering spectators.

Our concern was for the boat, however, and while people looked on we got in the water to keep her facing the shore while the winds and waves pushed the stern around and crushed the starboard outrigger against her unfortunate neighbour, which was not moored but bound up as solidly immobile as a house on its trestle and could not move away. *Sari*'s bow came around too and the whole bamboo outrigger pushed at it as we all lined up along it to push back.

This ineffectual defence had to be abandoned suddenly as the outrigger seemed about to crush us against the smaller boat. I ducked under it to avoid being strangled and tried to pull it away from the other side. Chico received a blow on the head as the outrigger slapped down, and he gave up the struggle momentarily as he seemed about to pass out. We continued to try to restrain her from safer positions, but the wayward vessel insisted on crashing the outrigger down over and over again on a sharp stake. The large bamboo we had scraped of paint and bound on with such care cracked and splintered, leaving a large hole to breach the outrigger's buoyancy.

The struggle continued until the squall had passed and I do not recall every manoeuvre, rope trick or act of heroic folly from the crew and the fishermen who had come to help, but the *Sarimanok* continued her frenzied flailing like a mad person and we had not succeeded in applying a straitjacket by the time the evil spirit of the weather which motivated her subsided a little. It was only a slight lull but it was enough for the ropes to be unleashed, the motor started, and a dash made for the padded cell of open water, where she could continue her rabid ragings cushioned from harm.

Bob's face during the fight was stamped with anguish at the possible destruction of his beloved boat. The frail deck had almost broken my leg when a slat gave way and trapped my shin on the run, and Steve had crashed through it right up to the thigh. Along with Chico's near concussion and similar injuries all round, we really felt we had been in a war as the clouds finally thinned and left only the rain for us to contend with. The men who had helped squatted on deck, shivering in their sarongs, their dark skins glossed with water. We remained with them, getting wetter and colder, but unable or unwilling to waste our dry clothes until all likelihood of getting soaked again had passed.

Don recovered quickly and stoked up a fire somehow with the damp wood. We all gulped down the tea he made as if we had just crossed a desert instead of being soaked by a storm.

'*Teh?*' Don offered our helpers too.

'*Tidak bisa,*' the Indonesian men said. 'We cannot.'

'*Puasa,*' they proclaimed, explaining in a single word that they were fasting for Ramadan. We knew that they should not touch food or drink, or even swallow their saliva during daylight, and we had considered this before tempting them, but surely they could let themselves off under such exceptional circumstances? They were adamant that they would not transgress, however, and watched without a flicker of envy as we devils in the wilderness drank our fill.

The bumping of the boat as she rose on the tide next morning was followed by much moving about of anchors like a game of chess over the sea bed, but eventually it was decided the best course was to bring her in to the beach again, but far away from other boats. The sails and bolt-ropes were brought out again, and new outriggers and steering oar were sought.

The timber for these took some finding, but Bob was soon as much a part of this village as he had been in the others and managed to track down the best materials. He worked for hours under the shady palms on the beach and held court with his Indonesian cronies who listened spellbound or exchanged boat-building stories with him. My Indonesian was not up to knowing exactly what he was saying, but I knew how well he could hold an audience in English and could see that he was giving 'good value'.

Smiley and Steve went off in the ducky to the nearest city of Kota Bahru. They did not return the next day, and a local policeman told us he had heard over the two-way radio that they were in prison. They were not stupid enough to do anything illegal during the expedition, but it did not quieten our fears and we were overjoyed, a couple of days later, to see them returning in a motor-powered boat, towing the Metzler behind. They had reached the town in five hours, and spent two days getting back.

'The motor went kaput again,' Steve explained.

'Yis, then we got lost in all these fish traps,' Smiley continued.

The shallow shelves around these islands are forested with wooden frameworks of poles from which nets are hung in a way that allows fish in but not out. Most have a small hut above the highest water level. Those we could see in the space between the islet and 'our' island were a strange sight, like giant spiders guarding the narrow waterway, made more intimidating by their wobbling reflection below.

'We climbed up on to one and slept there until the fisherman came to empty the net,' Steve took up the story again, 'and in the morning he called over the launch to drop us off home on the way.'

'He wasn't half surprised to see us there. Musta thought we'd come to steal his ruddy tucker,' said Smiley.

'It was scarey going between those traps in the dark, eh Smiles? Really spooky like a village with nobody in it. And when we got the lift back we couldn't remember the name of this place!' Steve declared, laughing with relief at their safe return.

The boat, clothed in palm fronds to keep the outriggers from drying out and cracking, was pushed out on the second attempt on the high tide. The chances to do this were few now before the waning moon would leave us high and dry with the neap tide. I did not want to go. This was better than tourist-ridden Bali! The children were quite restrained and did not bother us half so much as the Sulawesi kids had done, although we were even more of a novelty here. We would never have got here without our own vessel, and I would have preferred to stay in our endearingly blemished paradise a bit longer.

But the show must go on – and on and on – and after one false start when the new steering oar support framework was found to be riddled with faults, we made the nearest thing to a beeline that we could effect across the sea to the densely populated heart of the country: Java.

After nearly crashing head-on with a large fishing boat as we escaped from the dangerous coast, the days passed in a haze of frequent rain, soaking everyone including the cook and fire, and progressively stodgy meals of rice and noodles as the fish was used up. The boat's snake-like slithering over the swells gave way to the side-on rocking whenever the motor was not working and we could not head against the east wind. The new steering oar broke, and we risked broken fingers to put the other in its seating.

The rig up of the steering oar had been substantially changed and the new wooden structure was found to be worse, needing constant retightening by knocking wedges into gaps widened by the wangling motion of the oar. We were trying to move diagonally across the swells to get to the south-west, which made helm duty exhausting. The oar had to be turned so the narrow edge cut through each swell, since a rush of water on the broad side would bend it alarmingly and lift the supporting rig further off the deck. If left alone the oar would align itself in the path of least resistance, but to navigate successfully, we had to use strong-arm methods to coax it into giving a reasonable heading.

There was some argument among the experienced sailors about how the new rig should be adjusted, and hours of alterations

went on, bobbing on the Java Sea, drifting to the west away
from our goal.

Wednesday, 27th June
Up late at 7.30am. Had to concentrate on the steering to keep
turning the oar so that it will not uproot the rig, or jump out
of the notch. The watches have come full circle and I am back
with Bob on eight to twelve which, because of other duties which
keep him awake for many of his 'off-duty' hours, means three
or even four hours on the helm at a time. With the motion
making me feel sick, I sometimes leave the helm trembling and
weak to do my statutory twenty-five or thirty buckets of bailing.

Bailing takes over whenever the ingenious pump, like a vertical
'Bullworker', is blocked or otherwise incapacitated – which is most
of the time. To make sure that each watch does their fair share,
the number of buckets is fixed, though I have to double this
since I can only raise about half a bucketful. A better gauge is
the company's emblem printed on the ducky paddle that's stored,
blade downward, in the bilge water.

'Somebody hasn't done their bailing,' Steve accused as he took
over the watch. 'I can't see the elephant!' and the culprit, Smiley,
came over to find the picture of the trumpeting beast almost
submerged.

'Awww. Go on! He'll be right. There's his trunk,' he pointed
out.

'Yes. It looks as though he's using it as a snorkel,' was Steve's
parting shot.

I found out today why the duck we were given days ago has
still not been killed. José says it's unlucky to kill it at sea, so
now we have to keep tripping over it and clearing up its mess.
The poor thing is suffering even more than we are. It is tied by
one leg near the edge of the starboard outrigger deck, seasick and
unable to stand up in the awful motion of the boat. 'Donald' also
often falls overboard, plunged head first under each swell, which,
being a fresh-water bird, he doesn't like. Each time he is dragged
up again from the sea by the motion of the boat, he quacks loudly
in complaint and someone has to rescue him. Usually it's Chico,
whose bunk is nearest.

Thursday, 28th June
Up late again. Bob said I could stay in bed a bit longer. There was
more fiddling with the rudder oar. It was choppy and I was on the
helm all morning. I'm really feeling the need for a bit of exercise. A
good brisk walk would be nice. Chico was unusually snappy today,
he must be tired.

Friday, 29th June
It's *Hari Raya* (Great Day), meaning the end of the Muslim's
fasting month of Ramadan. José is ill again and hardly eating. I
feel a bit seasick. It's very rough. Bob was rather worried when he
saw a big storm ahead, but it missed us, thank goodness.

Saturday, 30th June
Bob offered halfway through our watch to come out and take over.
It was raining, which I sometimes find preferable to a merciless sun
beating down. I was enjoying an unheard singsong, however, and
was as wet as I could possibly get, so I carried on a while longer.
When the watch changed, Don drew my attention to Chico, who
was hunched over the tiller in the rain. His face was almost grey
and he sat with stony-faced endurance.

'Doesn't he look old out there?' Don asked, and I had to admit
that he did. Perhaps the strain of this voyage has changed him a
little each day, and I only saw it today because his tan had faded
and he looks bedraggled. It's awful to see him actually looking older
than he is.

There are a few islands in this stretch to avoid, and storms in
the distance are a perpetual worry. The engine is still often 'crook'
and Steve is constantly repairing it. Even when it is working, it can
often not be used because it splutters and gurgles as the swell covers
it, then revs up angrily like an electric saw with nothing to cut when
the propeller is lifted by the boat's motion out of the water.

We've been keeping a lookout for the lights of Surabaya, Java's
second city. A bright moon rising fooled us last night, but the lights
really are visible tonight, only the wind is holding us off. Bob and
Steve pumped up the ducky, put on the sputtering engine and
chased after a fishing vessel making for the port. I was worried they
would not be able to find their way back, but Steve took a compass

bearing on our position, and after nightfall they got within range by compass, then homed in on our light. The ship was carrying fish and could not wait to tow us as the load would go bad before they could land it.

Bob and I spent our watch fixing the motor support bracket, which is cracked. When Chico got up, a towel wrapped around his neck like a scarf, he seemed to have a very bad cold so I offered to stay up instead, but he wouldn't hear of it. It seems cold tonight, and after so many days of rain our warm clothes are all damp.

The morning brought new hope. The sun shone, the sail was hoisted and we landed on Java at last. We had not drifted very far but were some distance to the west of Surabaya. We were caught by fishermen when our weak old rope broke, and later towed into the harbour of Sedayulawas (or Sedayu, as it was known locally). The contrast with the neat island we had recently left could not have been more startling. It was like taking a ride into an untidy ships' graveyard, the dull scruffy boats tied to each other by a tangle of ropes along which rats could be seen moving house at night (we feared to gain more, but in fact lost our lonely rodent here), while the masts of sunken boats showed above the surface.

The trip into town was a joy, however. With the end of Ramadan, houses were thrown open to all comers with biscuits, snacks and drinks constantly on offer as a reaction to the daytime fast that had been their religious burden over the previous thirty days.

When Bob set out for Surabaya the next day, he climbed down into the unsteady canoe that was waiting to take him ashore dressed in the white trousers and shirt which he somehow always managed to clean perfectly after muddy market jaunts, holding his briefcase and respectable cream-coloured shoes. The slovenly scene of the harbour no longer seemed his domain at all and I hoped he would not have a twenty yard trudge through the mud to tarnish the spotless image.

Chico had taken to his bed with a constant headache just before we reached Java and I thought he must have 'flu. While Bob was in the city, however, he recovered slightly, partly because of a feeling of indispensability. Throughout the morning, he chiselled out a better niche for the steering oar in its rig, but the hard work made him dizzy and he was lying down again by the time Bob returned from Surabaya. He rose once more to join Bob in entertaining the fishermen who had towed us in but soon retired to bed as if paralytically drunk on a thimbleful of grog. I helped him in, afraid he would fall headlong off the boat, and he told me again he should marry me. 'Not on your life!' I told him unsympathetically. That would be going too far!

Market and shower trips on shore, the same old things, occupied the days. I hired a bicycle *becak* back from the market in the neighbouring town, where I saw a plethora of eye infections and the first beggars since Manila. The driver chatted me up over my head from the moment I boarded the machine (in which the passenger sits in a seat in front of the handle bars), but it was not until we were coasting down a hill that he told me he had no brakes.

'Why not!' I shouted accusingly over my shoulder, afraid to take my eyes from the vehicles coming up in the middle of the road.

'No need!' he assured me as we gathered speed with a long slope still in store for us. 'Got bell, see!' which, with my head facing the direction of any impending disaster, I did not, so he tinkled a tocsin for me like a Venetian gondolier serenading his signorina. Eventually he jumped off and stopped the machine. With each encounter with the Indonesian roads I liked them less, and was looking forward to getting back to the comparative safety of the sea.

That night we were embarrassingly grounded across the exit channel after a hit-and-run vessel had broken the front of an outrigger and the bowline. 'Hi there!' rang incongruously through the air as three figures climbed aboard. Don's parents, Mary and Harvey, were introduced, along with Bobby Lou, a friend of Chico's from Hawaii. They had been waiting two weeks in Bali for our scheduled arrival and had flown to Surabaya when Don had phoned telling of the delays.

The appearance of the vivacious, pretty Bobby Lou seemed to be a shock to Chico (as, in a different way, it was to me). She wanted him to leave the boat and stay with her until The Big One next year, and they sat together rather subdued in a silent battle of wills, Chico insisting on seeing this part of the voyage through to the end.

The next day was American Independence day, but the Hawaiians ignored this as they made the most of their few hours with us. I did not speak much to the visitors, leaving them to those they had come to see, and in no time the two women were away again with an 'aloha', pleased that they would be reunited with the men for a few months before the Indian Ocean voyage.

Don's father sailed on along the coast with us for the next twenty-four hours to share some of his son's experience. The harbour exit was filled with yachts and I steered with great care through the regatta, reliving the first days of the voyage through Harvey's enjoyment of the sailing and the novelty of our craft. Motoring through a collection of fish traps at night, all hands were needed on deck to weave a safe passage through the obstacle course, and with Chico on the helm, sicker than he admitted, we did well to get off without a single hit. In the glow from the few remaining workable torches the spindly structures rose up quickly and menacingly close from the dark, and the instructions first given in correct nautical terms like 'hard a-port!' gave way rapidly to 'left quick!' After a veritable suburban sprawl of these objects, we reached the rural spaces again.

'How close are we to land?' Bob asked the navigator.

'*Al-lah huwa al-'akbar!*' the muezzin's call to prayer wafted over to us, and the crowing of a cock was clearly audible in the stillness.

'Close enough!' Steve replied with a laugh as he dropped the anchor to hold us until the light of morning.

8. *Aloha*

I was worried about Chico. On the helm through the fish traps he had nearly brought us to disaster several times by turning the wrong way, or reacting slowly, and afterwards when he took the water I had boiled to make cocoa, it was nearly cold by the time the job was finished. He had been uncharacteristically peevish for some time, and his bright eyes showed clearly he had a fever.

He lay in bed and, when I woke, I saw he had night-time shivers. I scrounged blankets from everyone to pile layer upon layer over him in a futile attempt to warm him. It looked like malaria, but he had backache too, which made Don and Bob, who had suffered from it, think it was dengue or 'breakbone' fever.

'It's awful but you don't die of it!' we said waggishly to jolly him along, but the fatality rate of an illness is not the only consideration, and Chico was suffering immensely. He needed help to drink and could not eat. An outing to urinate over the side was dangerous and he took to kneeling on his bunk to relieve himself through the window. It took him quarter of an hour to raise himself on his side, curve his stiff back sufficiently to climb through the window and sit on the deck where Bob lavished an hour's care on bathing him and putting on a clean shirt to make him feel better.

Harvey left us at the industrial area of Surabaya to rush home on business after a hair-raising journey through the heavy shipping of the dock area. He was sorry not to be able to say *ciao* to Chico, who by now seemed to be sleeping much of the time, wrapped in a space blanket and wearing a woolly hat in the heat of the day.

We virtually stopped and looked both ways before crossing the path of the ferry to Madura, the large island off the north-east of Java, and tied up in the little channel where the boats were boarded. Steve, Smiley and I went ashore and, returning with a carton of ice cream from the first supermarket we had seen in months, and grated ice from the quayside *es campur* vendor, we then continued around the coast, in spite of misgivings about Chico's condition. He was a little delirious, not able to rest until his filthy old cap was clutched to his chest when it began to rain, as if it was a treasure which should not get wet. I felt we should take the opportunity of being in the city to get medical advice. Bob was keen to move on, however, and feeling intimidated by his urgency I did not insist.

The difficulty of finding a passage between Java and Madura occupied the next hour or two, and when, after settling him down, Chico kept hold of my hand with his hot one, I had to pull it away to get up to continue my work. The contact I had been longing for was there, but I rejected it just when he needed me most. I felt shame and remorse even as I hurried away. When Bob came to offer Chico some ice cream, he was lying on his back, staring with a dazed expression on his face. Bob held a spoon to his mouth and, though a little remained on his lower lip, most of the ice cream was untasted. He had not licked any off the spoon, and when Bob shone a torch in his eyes the pupil contraction reflex was absent too.

Everyone not held at their post was watching him now, kneeling on bunks or with head and shoulders pushed through a window. As if for his attentive fans, Chico then gave a performance which made my flesh creep. His body stiffened, his arms jerked and, as he groaned, froth appeared between his lips. We needed a doctor desperately now and bitterly reproached ourselves for leaving the city behind.

Docking at the next village, Bob and Steve went off in the ducky to arrange for an ambulance, while I packed a small bag for Chico as darkness fell. Time dragged on. I came close to listen for his breathing every minute, feeling his heat through his thin shirt. The men returned with a stretcher on to which he was manhandled as gently as possible, then tied on to prevent him sliding off as he was passed with difficulty out on deck and down onto the ducky, bobbing out of phase with *Sari*.

The ropes served also to control the fit that shook him as we neared the shore, but the boat rocked with the violence of it and Steve and Bob splashed off with him to the shore while I waded under the pilings to tie up the boat. The situation was so grave that I could not take it seriously, and Bob's attempts at conversation in the police van to the hospital in Surabaya showed his awe at the predicament.

The casualty department of the hospital was full but we were seen quickly. Bob and I stood in solidarity for once, quibbling about the draught from the window on the sweating patient being examined in the corridor, and taking it in turns to try and convince the immigration men who appeared from nowhere that our visas were in order. Each time I was called away through the swing doors in the corridor to be questioned about the matter – so trivial under the circumstances – I kept running back to look through the partition so that I could help if any problem arose. I was exasperated almost to the point of being insolent to the dull-witted soldier who seemed to consider the rubber stamps in Chico's passport more important than his life.

It was more than an hour before Chico was put to bed with the equipment which we lucky foreigners could afford to buy from the basement pharmacy. There were dextrose and antibiotic drips putting fluid in and a urine bag collecting the little that came out. When he had another fit in the corridor, which seemed to be caused by great efforts to breathe when his bronchi were blocked, Bob and I turned him on his side and the offending mucus dripped on to the trolley and floor. Paper tissues and a suction apparatus were brought, and the farcical attempts we made to force the outdated piece of equipment to suck rather than blow would have seemed funny if our need of it had not been so great.

Bob and I stayed with Chico the first night. Now that he was in a hospital bed, things seemed brighter, and we conspired together in the darkened ward like schoolboys having a midnight feast. The night brought more seizures, and we jumped up from our floor space to assist with his breathing. Next morning, I sat at the coffee stall outside the hospital gates, miserable but still hopeful that a solution could be found. During the day, Bob did the rounds of American Consulate, port authorities and immigration office, while I stayed at Chico's bedside.

Even now we were providing entertainment. The visitors of the other patients were curious to see a Western patient and even peered between the curtain I pulled around him as their prurience became too much. The men were the worst, flirting quite openly when they found the patient was not my husband, as if they did not notice my concern.

The cats prowling the wards were disconcerting, but preferable I suppose (in spite of the faeces they had no choice but to drop under the beds) to the rats, mice and cockroaches they were keeping at bay.

Morning and evening, bowls of water were provided for washing patients in bed and I used one the first time it was offered. Though I tended Chico's body, it was only a container which would not show the treasures it guarded. How awful it would be if he knew what was happening to him and how unjust that the malfunction of this machine made up for two penn'orth of chemicals could hold a person's whole earthly existence to ransom.

The poor doctors suffered from my haranguing and, after the usual rapid ward rounds, they made quickly for the door, while I, snatching up the Indonesian dictionary from the bedside table, hurried for the other door, vaulting an empty bed in my path, to waylay them in the corridor. The replies were always the same. They were doing all they could, but still did not know what the illness was. I hoped that Bob was having some success finding help elsewhere.

'Don't die! We love you,' I repeated, barely audibly, not daring to make the remark more personal even though he seemed unconscious, as I watched his half-open eyes obsessively for any flicker of recognition.

When he returned, Bob encouraged him without restraint.

'Come on, Chico, hang on. Don't leave us before the job's finished, you bastard!' which was, in effect, what I had been telling him all along. He told me more quietly, as he stood at the foot of the bed and surveyed the wreck his friend had become, 'He mustn't die. I *love* him!' And he did.

Bob found the Peace Corps doctor, Dr Rusdiah, through the United States Consulate. On Sunday afternoon I was relieved of duty at the bedside for a few hours and was taken off to the doctor's house to rest while Bob took over, but I could not sleep. When Bob later followed the doctor into the comfortable living room, he gave me a look of despair behind his back, and whispered, 'He thinks its encephalitis now, and there's no way they can cure it here.'

The doctor had earlier thought it might be meningitis, and I suspected cerebral malaria. There is some hope of deliverance from those diseases in Indonesia, but it was now imperative to get Chico out of the country. Bob made good use of the telephone which Dr Rusdiah generously bestowed upon him during the night to ring everyone he knew who might be able to help from the USA to Australia, while I returned to tend Chico again.

Though I could do little to help, I leapt up time and again during the night for the noisy aspiration equipment, hoping that I was helping rather than torturing him. His difficulty with breathing was probably due to his smoking, but the doctors, casting about for a reasonable diagnosis so they could begin effective treatment, pounced upon it as the cause of his illness. When the technicians returned from their weekend break soon after midnight, they came down the sleeping ward in procession with an impressive-looking machine to X-ray Chico's lungs.

After waiting since Saturday night for the technicians' help in diagnosing the illness, the futility of X-raying lungs at the possible expense of more suffering for Chico, exasperated me to tears. I danced about in agitation and exhorted them, as quietly as I could, 'It's his head that needs looking at. X-ray his head, why don't you?'

'We have instructions to do a chest X-ray,' said one technician as he consulted an official-looking form, and if they valued their jobs, that is what they had to do.

Later that morning I followed Chico's trolley along corridors, down lifts and across yards until I was quite lost. The sparkling clean department where we stopped had a battery of fearsome-looking machines with which he could be 'defibrillated'. Dr Karyadi was kind and helpful, explaining that it would improve his breathing, but while I was pleased they were aiding his immediate survival, I could not help wishing they could concentrate on the primary symptoms of the illness.

Though I had been looking at his face almost constantly for thirty-six hours, I now realised I had only been scanning his features and not looking at him. Now he had been taken to a place I could not enter, and as I pressed my face to the glass, I guessed there would never be another chance.

Bob saw that he was being well looked after and I was swept away, almost reluctantly, to sit in the air-conditioned comfort of the US Consulate while Bob sent telexes and made more phone calls. The Americans were also trying to have Chico moved and, after a night and a day of endeavour, a deal was clinched. The US military at Clarke Airbase in the Philippines agreed to fly over a medically equipped plane to take him to their hospital near Manila. This concession, so laboriously won by Bob, was finally granted in deference, no doubt, to Chico's active service in Korea in the fifties, a terrible period of his life that only now reaped some kind of reward.

I dashed back to the boat, which had been brought to the city under Steve's command and now lay dwarfed among the merchant and passenger vessels anchored in the straits between Java and Madura. There, I threw a bag of things together for Bob, who had somehow managed to get Chico's passport back from immigration and was to accompany him to the Philippines. I delivered the bag to him at the hospital where I clasped Chico's gold chain around his neck. I had been wearing it in case anyone should try to steal it while I was not at the bedside. It seemed a trivial thing, but Chico valued the present from his brother and wore it constantly.

A deep sleep was broken by the sound of panic on deck.

'Oh, please, let them not need me,' I prayed and drowsed on a bit. I had hardly slept for about sixty hours and my leaden limbs would not move. But I knew the noise was not going to go away on its own, and I crawled out on deck to find out what the problem was.

The metal anchor could not hold us in the rush of water in the straits and we were drifting west. Smiley zipped over on the inflatable to the nearest safely anchored boat, marked on the side as *Scrap*, to tie on a line. In the morning the arrangement seemed fine, but during the two weeks that we were to spend off Tanjung Perak in Surabaya, many nights were broken by struggles to stop *Sari* crushing an outrigger and tipping over.

Most of the time there was a very strong current through the straits which kept us streaming well out behind the other boat, but with the twice daily tide changes the problems began. When trailing out to the west, things were usually fine because the tide and wind carried us in the same direction. One might feel a small jolt and look out from bed or up from work on the deck to see the metal ship comfortably nestled between our hull and an outrigger, the stern nudging gently at *Sari*'s *batangan*. A single push at the rusty hulk was all that was needed to separate us.

When the tide changed to charge us from the west, however, the wind continued to blow from the east, and we were crushed against the ship by the onslaught of the current. The best we could do was to keep pushing and holding off until the tide had turned completely, and that fortnight was speckled with these ugly scenes of fear, one night being almost crushed between our ship and another which was anchored too close. We fended off both boats again and pursued our own dark thoughts in the black night until the danger was over.

Albrecht Schaefer, the German journalist who had visited us in Languyan, found us early on the morning after my return from the hospital. He was aching to be part of the expedition too and I told him he should tackle Bob at the next opportunity. Chico would not now be taking part in the next year's sailing, no matter how well he recovered.

The town of Surabaya was large and busy, but infinitely preferable to Jakarta. There was a sign on one main road proclaiming the city to be the home of 'HEROIC, SMILING, FRIENDLY PEOPLE' and the last two adjectives certainly applied. Each day, as I went out on various errands to new parts of the city, I had only to walk to the *bemo* station by the port and ask the drivers and passengers the way, and they would ponder for a second then vie with each other to tell me the best route and which *bemos* to take.

After taking leave of Albrecht, I went off to the nearest laundry, cushioned in the stinking pile of linen in the front of a three-wheeled bicycle *becak*. My return to the boat, driving myself across the fast flow of vessel and current in the inflatable, was the last moment of hope. Don tied up the painter to the port deck and extended the same welcoming hand with which he had helped me back after my unexpected dip between Sulawesi and Borneo.

'Chico died this morning at 9am,' he told me quietly as soon as I was safely on board. My mind circled around the enquiry, 'our time or theirs?' as if it was imperative to pinpoint the exact moment.

'So much for palm reading,' I thought. So much too for his copious plans for the future.

Marie, the secretary from the US Consulate, had brought the telex from Bob over to the boat, and Don showed it to me. The cause was hepatitis and kidney failure, and no mention was made of the other illnesses suspected. Even this bit of paper in my hand could not turn the knowledge of what had happened into fact for me.

Steve and Smiley soon returned but the telling of the news to them made it no more acceptable. They registered their sorrow, but their true feelings did not show. Obviously they could not really believe it either.

Getting up in the night for a struggle with *Sari* was sheer misery now that it dumped on us more time in which to rake over the infertile soil of speculation over whether Chico would have survived if he had gone home with Bobby Lou, or if we had treated his ''flu' with more concern and got an earlier diagnosis.

Bob later blamed Chico's illness on the drinking water picked up from our lovely island off Borneo, but in fact all our provisions were suspect and we were foolish enough, right from our days in the Philippines, to drink unboiled water. Like walking barefoot outside, this was something I questioned on my arrival, but I soon fitted in with the habit. I therefore felt guilty, as did Bob, that our neglect could have caused Chico's death.

José's insistence on keeping the dirty duck alive for ten days so as not to bring bad luck upon us had failed spectacularly and might even have been the cause of the misfortune, infecting Chico with the virus. José had taken some care of Chico when he first became sick, wrapping the hurriedly piled blankets tenderly around him and taking care to cover his feet, but had mostly ignored him. I was appalled by his apparent unconcern at the death, but this was probably due to his more intimate acquaintance with it.

Marie wrote a poem for Chico, which moved Bob to praise her sensitivity, but I felt they were both deluding themselves. How gratifying it must be to express noble sentiments for a stranger whose death gave a sort of pang but no real pain. How indulgent to wallow in a delicious melancholy of grief by proxy. Everyone sympathised with Chico's family and friends, and with Bob, whose long friendship with him was known and whose attachment plain to see, but no one knew how much I cared for him. I could not divulge this now that his death made the admission suspect and I wanted to shout out, 'What about me? Who's going to comfort me?'

Bob returned larger than life like Santa Claus, distributing PAL tickets and T-shirts. He became more sombre in a moment, though, when he came across the death certificate in his brief case. The classic signs of hepatitis A – dark urine, yellow skin and eyewhites – had only appeared on the hospital plane and he must have felt again the chill of his last few hours with Chico.

One of Chico's many friends tried to find some solace in going to the undertakers to be near him, and Bob found her behaviour 'strange', but I understood completely the wish to see him again. Perhaps she would envy me the dreadful time I spent with him in hospital, but I knew from that experience that the mere presence of his body without the spark of life gave no deliverance from pain. He had been cremated now, and I could not bear to think that a pile of ashes was all that was left of the beautiful body which had sometimes made me weak in the knees.

I tried to tell Bob how I felt I had missed getting to know Chico well.

'You are privileged to have known him at all,' Bob replied, but as if sensitive to my special feeling for him, he removed the gold chain I had put around his neck for safe keeping.

'I think Chico would have wanted you to have this,' he said indulgently as he offered it to me at arm's length. I trembled lest the trinket glittering in the lamplight should slip from his hand and through the deck to the dark sea below. It was not really his to give, but I was touched at his sacrifice of a memento he must have coveted himself and I grasped it firmly, with enormous gratitude.

We still had a long way to go. We continued using a 'long tail' motor the men had bought for the rest of the journey. The little outboard could not cope alone with the head winds and the noxious fuel of the newcomer soon coated our mouths from the frequent syphoning, and made the deck around it slippery.

The shaft broke and José fixed it several times. A wing snapped off the propellor and we took an eventful magical mystery tour in the dark to find replacements in the lively town of Pasuruan. The outriggers had become slimy as a result of our not being able to get down to clean them in the 'rapids' of Surabaya, and the frequent encounters with *Scrap* had worn away some of the rattan so the outriggers needed relashing. Back in caustic form, Bob reproached us for our two weeks' 'holiday' in Surabaya, forgetting the deck repairs and searches for the new motor.

In short, things seemed to be back to normal, but the effect was only superficial. The whole mood of the expedition was changed. Bob was grieving secretly, and everyone cherished a souvenir of Chico.

Within five days we had a friendly encounter with the Muslim stronghold of Singaraja on the north coast of the Hindu island of Bali, and made the passage through part of the fast flowing Lombok Straits. The famous whirlpools of one bay on Bali are a constant threat which Steve and Bob brought us through unscathed, and we sailed triumphantly into our winter quarters on the east coast of Bali, sporting our PAL T-shirts proudly like a mariner's uniform.

There was a festival all over Bali which is celebrated only every twenty years, and wherever we went on the island we could not help but be drawn in. But desolation afflicted us, and, as Steve said, no half hour had passed since Chico's death without a thought of him. Bob was his usual obstreperous self when he had been drinking, but on my way back to the boat late one afternoon I was called to the upstairs room of the hotel where he was said to be insulting the Chinese management and 'throwing furniture from the balcony'.

When I arrived, only a clothes horse had gone over the edge, but the scene in the room was comical. Steve and Smiley, and several of the hotel staff, were reasoning with him, but from a distance as if he were a savage animal. I joined them, but a deal to pay for the damage was already negotiated. Bob tied up his bundle of 'firewood' with care, and we brought him safely to the street. He was not going to come home with us, and the others left me with him saying, 'Stop him doing anything silly.'

'What do you expect me to do?' I asked. 'He's bigger than me.' There was no answer to that, but they were tired of the whole incident.

'Just watch him,' Smiley suggested, and I did for a while, though for what purpose I was not sure. He had swum back to our boat in an unsteady state the night before, but knew his own capabilities even now, and my fear was mainly for the bad impression he would make in a town in which he meant to spend months renewing the *Sarimanok*. I trailed him for a few minutes as he thought up more mischief and poured scorn on my chaperoning until, realising my presence was just a further irritation, I left him to roam and mourn in peace.

I delighted in the beauty of Bali, but every green vista of terraced hills and every swim in crystal streams was tainted by the knowledge that Chico would not see or paint them now. I watched with envy the freedom with which the tourists in Bali changed partners and, although I did not want to be like that, realised that if I had taken their easy path just once I would not be feeling so remorseful now.

In five months I had got to know Chico well enough to know what I was missing. I would never know him properly now and felt sick with jealousy for those who had been close. The pain I felt was more for my own bereavement than for his forfeit of life, but grief is selfish, and soon after reaching the safety of Bali, I was convulsed by a wild fit of sobbing on the deck, not caring who would hear.

Part three
Better to travel hopefully?

9. Present continuous tense

When I returned to Bali in March, it seemed a different place
from the one I had left the previous October, though little had
really changed except for the structure of the *Sarimanok*. Under
her modesty wraps of canvas I saw that the bow and stern had
been built up so that the gunwale rose above the level of the deck
– good news for the helmsman – and the new outriggers lay beside
her ready for binding on with rattan. I did not inspect the inside but
noticed that a graffiti exhortation 'DO NOT SMOKING' remained
on her beams. She looked at home, like a mother hen surrounded
by smaller double-outrigger canoes (*jukungs*) with long open beaks
protruding in front, bulging eyes on the bow to search for danger,
and ears carved behind them to hear it.

I had meant to continue travelling in the eastern islands of
Indonesia after our land journey to the village of Lamalera in
the eastern islands where whales are still caught by men who
jump on to their backs to harpoon them. I did so for a while,
but I could not appreciate the beauty of the world. More than
anything, I craved privacy, which would never be allowed by these
gregarious people.

At home I spent the winter researching the diet of the migrants,
grieving and worrying, so that it was with a feeling of relief at
facing the journey at last that I returned to Indonesia in February.
By the time I reached Bali I felt enthusiastic about the voyage
again.

'Hi, Sal!' Bob greeted me as I approached the circular sunshade
like a bandstand, which we called the 'wind house'. He hugged
me and I felt hypocritical as I returned the pressure, but entered
into the spirit of the moment, resolving once again to start with a
clean slate.

'Steve's been here since January and done *nothing*!' he alleged.
I knew Bob by now and was sure this was an exaggeration, but
I understood Steve too and was confident he would 'deliver the
goods' once again when he was in his element at sea.

Professor Bill McGrath, the new navigator for the ocean crossing,
had just arrived. He was in his sixties, tall and rather thin, with
sparse, greying hair, but his lilting American accent and confidence
were reassuring. I soon learnt that his naval experience had led him
to appreciate the need for as much water as we could carry. I had
found an ally!

During a visit to Bob's friend, Father Franz Lackner, on the
small island of Savu the previous year, my leg infections (one of
which had become a deep ulcer) finally healed, but old wounds
were opened in my mind by Franz's concern for our safety.
Bob did not seem willing to take excess drinking water and
had arrived on Franz's shores during an earlier expedition with
almost none. This was the disaster I feared most. On my return
home I therefore searched (in vain) for a cheap, small desalinator
we could take for emergencies, and mentioned water in a letter
to Bob.

This prompted the assertion that we would not take any such
namby-pamby machines, coupled with the preposterous statement
that we could suck water from fish in an emergency as Bombard
had done (never mind that we were unlikely to catch enough fish
anyway). The observation that 'Water . . . is not a problem' caused
me to heap all sorts of imprecations upon him in a letter which I
then thought better of sending.

Steve too clasped me to his chest for a moment before we fell
immediately to discussing the necessity of preventing the boat from
taking the waves beam-on this year. The swells could be thirty feet
high and, though Bill pointed out that the smaller the boat, the
better it can take big seas, she would soon tip over if she met them
like a stubborn crab as she had before.

Steve was also concerned about water, and I felt happier that we
could show a united front if Bob refused to take the right steps to
ensure survival.

'I don't care about dying,' I said – a sentiment not apparently
shared by the others – 'but I don't want to die slowly of thirst or
end up with damaged kidneys like Bombard.'

Within a couple of days, Bob conceded that we should carry some water in bladders and jerry cans, but his calculation of our needs still seemed low and he blew his top like a volcano whenever the subject was broached again.

Poor Bob! His dream was of sailing to Madagascar from South-East Asia in a traditional craft like the ancestors, but he could not do it alone. He had to bring in others to help who *would* keep asking for compromises. He wanted us to wear only capes of palm leaf or bark to be traditional in dress as well as navigation, food and boat design, but we feared to be constantly wet and cold. He wanted to carry water in ceramic jars, but we pleaded for a plastic back-up because the poor quality unglazed jars of the island broke so easily. Bill had even asked Tom Vosmer of Tim Severin's *Sindbad* expedition to 'vet' the vessel for safety, and he had pronounced it good, though Bob cannot have liked this indictment of his own skill.

As Don and I had considered when mulling over the matter before, 'What Bob really needs is a clone of himself to do all the jobs on board.'

'He'd still argue with everyone,' we chuckled.

He did not seem to realise that, even following his blueprint for the perfect expedition, untrammelled by conflicting wills, he would eventually find necessary some concessions to survival. Having others trying to muscle in on the orchestration of his dream when he had invited them in only as mindless performers, however, must have cheated him of the untainted realisation of his artistic ideal. Other expeditions have the same problems, and their participants also slander the tyranny of their leaders. More than one crew member of a sailing expedition has backed out before or during the voyage. Experience with Bob and with Greg's departure convinced me this was not solely the manifestation of last-minute 'cold feet' over the sanity of an enterprise, but that personality differences inflict a greater torture than even fear can.

My typed list of traditional foods, which impressed Bob's girl-friend, Jacqui, by its 'professionalism', annoyed Bob by its genesis from speculation and extrapolation from known facts, when he wanted to deal in certainties. He increased my tension throughout the stay in Bali by periodically re-opening the subject of particular foods which I had already laid to rest as non-starters, and when I flew back to consult my notes he jeered that I did not retain volumes of facts in my head. He had dubbed me an 'expert' – a term I rarely use of anyone, least of all myself – then disparaged me for not living up to his ideal, sometimes marvelling that I did not seem to realise facts about food which 'everybody knows' when in fact he, like 'everybody', had got it wrong.

Jacqui refereed our arguments and told me I did not stand up to Bob enough, but she did not know the history of our relationship. I still feared to be left behind, but, more than that, I now realised that Bob thrived on conflict whereas I wilted before it. Victory was so easy for him that I refused to give him the chance to make a dunce out of me with his superior eloquence and spurious logic. If I took the kicks like a brick wall, his attacks would only be more satisfying. If I offered no gratifying resistance, he would soon tire of it. At least that was the theory, and it worked to some extent, though it also earned for me the reputation of a doormat.

I also confided in Jacqui my affection for Chico, whom she had known, and my remorse at not telling him of it. Some time after her departure Bob broached the subject, proving she had told him of our talk. He had not realised my attachment before, and from then on we were closer, as if I had at last been allowed into the hallowed precincts inhabited by Chico's close friends.

The bungalows we lived in were a place of pilgrimage to travellers who had heard about the expedition. Bob enjoyed holding court, repeating for the umpteenth time how the whole project had begun, and expounding his theories of the migrations where they differed from accepted doctrine. I admired enormously his capacity as ringmaster, and he saw off many a contented young traveller, fired with his enthusiasm for the voyage and smitten by a kind of hero-worship for him.

Our intentions on the island were the same as the previous year: constructing the boat, collecting food stores and learning the appropriate sailing skills before launching. But this was a tourist island and a Hindu one. The presence of other foreigners in abundance could be annoying, but it also gave the place a holiday atmosphere, while the unique religion of Bali is lived daily, whether the faithful are being observed or not. The happy and relaxed character of the people, so different from the repressive, submissive philosophy of Islam, was liberating.

For two months Bob had no money to spend on the provisions for the voyage and I experimented in preservation techniques and with the sprouting of root ginger and soya beans, which could be a source of vitamin C when this friable nutrient was in short supply on the ocean. I set up my laboratory on the patio of the bungalow I occupied alone – what heaven to have some privacy this time! – designing drying tables which Bob employed workmen to construct from bamboo.

Although I spoke some Indonesian, I was still shy about enlisting help. *Ibu* ('mother', the wife of the proprietor), was, however, very approachable and helped with advice on local food and how to dry it. From my porch, I watched the returning fishermen each morning, their multicoloured sails reflected in the calm morning water, and bought fish from their wives as soon as they had waded into the sea to unload the catch as the *jukung* was dragged up on shore.

I cut small drying trays from sleeping mats, and spent my mornings, after an early visit to the local market, cutting bananas and other fruit and vegetables into slices to the tune of the lapping sea and birds which made an odd whirring sound overhead, like interference around an electricity pylon.

In spite of clearer-cut duties and frequent outings this year, however, the three months spent in the heaven of Bali were diabolical inside my head. I felt renewed regret about Chico and my desolation swelled and receded like the tides. I soon realised the barrier between pain and relief is nebulous and I was still a long way from the shore.

No sooner had Jacqui left than Bob found another lady, Dagmar, who was enigmatic and tragic. He fell for her deeply, but soon after her departure took up with a string of passing fancies (one at a time), which I felt inclined to condemn until I saw that the women took his attentions in the same light-hearted, throw-away spirit in which he gave them.

I felt a kind of jealousy for the diversion of his attention from the project we shared, though he never neglected work for them and his liaisons were probably therapeutic. He bore his responsibility as expedition leader alone now, but he put on a brave show of strength. When the going was particularly rough his nervousness showed in his more than usually boisterous behaviour, however, and I tried to see him as vulnerable too.

He realised I was lonely as well, and intimidated by my responsibilities. One evening, seeing me looking gloomy, he stroked my
hair as he made for his typing table, and said, 'Never mind, Sal.
We'll make you the sexiest thing . . .', as if my lack of indulgence
with the opposite sex was because I was not attractive enough.

Although sensible of his wish to console, I was bubbling over
with fury at his assumption that fasting in the midst of plenty is
proof that the abstainer is not hungry or cannot find a plate! It
did not occur to him that chastity could be a person's reluctant
alternative to loveless sex. He did not understand either that a
long-awaited love having passed by, for me there was not another
just cresting the horizon like a rush-hour bus.

I wanted to explain and justify myself to him, but always
found him difficult to talk to, so I sent him a letter with a
few grouses. I regretted the childishness of it immediately. Bob
had always thought I was a sexless wimp, now he knew I was a
frustrated one.

Steve had already gone back to Australia for a while, and Bill
and Nettie, his lady friend, went to Singapore for a break. I liked
the couple and missed them. She had given advice and pointed
out a useful book she had found to help with my food list, and
Bill was a 'sweetie', helping in practical matters, complimenting
and indulging me like a child. He had been to sea often and was
convinced that women aboard raise the tone of a journey at sea. He
called me 'Albatross' not, as I first thought, because I was a burden
hung around the neck, but because he said I was graceful like the
soaring bird.

I was now 'alone' with Bob and went on a hired motorbike with
him to search for building materials or food, or to commission the
firing of water storage jars. Returning in the dark, singing at the
tops of our voices over the motor's growl, he scrutinised the road
ahead, poorly illuminated by the front lamp, as I struggled to keep
hold of the acquired tools and rattan, or cradle on my lap the yoke
from which swung gourds of palm vinegar.

Leaving the bungalows by the more solid back path one day, we
noticed the flying dark mane and slender form of a Spanish woman
we had not yet met, heading for trouble on the sandy beach road.

'Mmm! Wonder if there's room for her at the bungalows,' Bob
mused aloud so I could hear on the pillion seat.

'Oh dear! If not she'll probably have to share a room with someone,' I commiserated with stagey articulation and exaggerated concern.

'I wonder who that will be,' I continued in the same vein, and we sniggered like drinking mates eyeing up the female 'talent' in the pub.

As a woman I was treated differently from the other crew members and at such times as this realised with a shock to my 'liberated' pride that I appreciated it.

'Oh well,' I sighed, as I prepared to relinquish my seat on outings in the next few days. 'I'll just have resign myself to being one of the boys for a bit longer.'

Bob had to borrow money since the boat builders had to be paid and, though Bill McGrath was a source of funding, he could not be tapped forever. Bob's charm, after his journalistic earning power, was his most valuable asset and he used it to try to wheedle money out of everyone.

Some gave money knowing they might never get it back, simply because they saw the charismatic Bob as good value, providing as he did a uniquely entertaining interlude in their lives. When money was available, though, suddenly everything came up roses and Bob juggled his debts like a city financier, being equally cool about the quantities involved.

Before my return to Bali, Antonio Quijano, the Philippine shipwright, had been and gone. He had been brought down to direct the alterations to the *Sarimanok*, and the local men working on the vessel had shown a great deal of respect for his skill, but they were experienced themselves and worked well with little supervision. Following the previous year's steering oar problems, the new ones were gigantic – huge pieces of wood joined into larger ones by exquisite butterfly joints.

'Phew! Look at the size of those oars!' Bob exclaimed when he first saw one of these monsters, its tip resting at the bottom of a pit into which a man could sink up to the shoulder. This had been dug into the sand at the stern of the vessel to accommodate the long blade while it was tried for size in the helm rig. One was to be lashed in place to act as a dagger board, while the other, on the

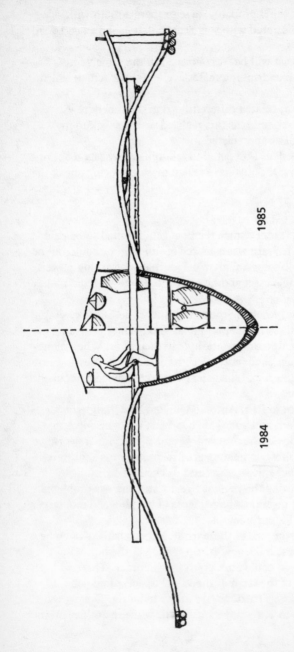

1985

1984

Section of the Sarimanok

starboard (which would be the leeside for our crossing), was to be fitted with a tiller for manipulation.

'They won't break, but the stern might with the force that thing will put on it,' he mused aloud.

Bob looked on with a mixture of pride and concern that in ironing out another of the problems of our sail down from Tawi Tawi, he might have created a greater one.

Yet another problem that troubled him for a long time was the carriage of the outriggers. The heavy bamboo poles, of which he planned to lash five on each side, had to be supported more firmly than the flexible S-connectors could do alone. When the solution finally hit him, he came back in exuberant mood from the building site on the beach.

'Listen to this, Sal!' he began. 'And *please* be enthusiastic for me,' he begged when he discerned I was in a despondent mood. 'I'm going to put extra beams over the *batangans* with supports down to the outriggers.'

I was not quite sure what he meant but tried to look bowled over by his ingenuity. I was genuinely impressed when he drew his plan, sketching the upward curve of the new pieces of timber, which grasped the 'hand grip' of cricket-bat-shaped timbers. The lower tip of the vertical bat was to be bound to the bamboo poles like the blade of a waiting batsman adhering to the crease. The springiness of curved beams was essential, but, after the difficulty of bending the S-connectors, he thought it better to use beams with a natural curve, and went off with renewed self-regard to search for some.

The masts were to be bipod this time, and he recalled how the whaling *pledangs* of Lamalera had masts which suffered none of the chafing of beams we had experienced. When Don returned to Bali en route for the whaling island, he asked him to note and photograph how they were constructed. I was pleased to see Don back in Bali, but after the statutory hug, we learned that he was returning almost immediately to the east to get those elusive pictures of a successful whale capture. I went later to buy the palm-weave sails they were making for us.

The last hour's walk into Lamalera was a relief after the teeth-rattling pillion motorbike journey through the forest from the north of the island. I was greeted by the children of the town, who remembered me from the previous year, and I was pleased to find Don still there. We went out in the *pledang* of one clan to hunt *ikan paus*, 'pope fish' or whales. None was caught, for which I was secretly, and rather selfishly, relieved, but I enjoyed the excitement of the chase and saw the dramatic dives that men on other boats made onto whales or onto the Manta rays whose dark forms 'flew' just beneath the surface like aquatic vampires with their cloaks flapping.

I also had the opportunity to watch how the boats were handled. When the wind was sufficient, the two-legged mast was unearthed from its recumbent resting place along the thwarts, placed astride the vessel and hauled up by the rope stays, with which it was secured in a forward raked position. As I copied the design, I marvelled at the simplicity of the ingenious wishbone structure which held the two legs of the mast together, the hollowness of its double cap allowing some movement of each pole while preventing them from rubbing each other. The stay ropes were looped over the tail of this inverted Y-shaped joint, keeping it down on the mast poles when in sailing stance, and the sail was hoisted by a halyard which ran through a hole in the Y-tail above the stay loops, preventing them from coming free from the mast if they should slacken.

The rectangular sails were seen in all their glory. Each square in the network of fine cord was individually woven with strips of dried *gebang* palm frond. The lattice-work opened slightly in strong wind, allowing the excess to sieve through. When a square was damaged, it could be cut out and new webbing worked in its place, as we had seen on the beach in the afternoons, giving the sail a chequered appearance of differently weathered and coloured rectangles.

We had asked the whalers to make us some palm-weave sails, but the shopkeeper who had been put in charge of the supervision of the sail weaving did not wield power over the appropriate people, and the promised payment being in one lump (to wit, an outboard motor) could not be divided between all families undertaking the task. It is not surprising, therefore, that the vast cord-net skeleton of the mainsail was only partly fleshed out with woven squares. We purchased it with cash, however, then strode the sea shore literally offering money for old rope.

Our ignorance of the correct price was a hindrance to our bargaining credibility. Having stretched out a rope and measured it, we tried to look sage as we pondered. The fishermen did not know the value of the resources and labour that went into their work either, and they did likewise. This game of double bluff was a comedy resulting in the purchase of scraggy lengths of line formerly attached to the large Manta ray harpoon heads for the same price as thick cables of whale-bearing strength, but when we left with our stash of ropes, as well as whale and ray meat, on the boat for Flores, the large island to the west, everyone seemed satisfied with their deals.

From Kupang, we collected the *gula air* (liquid sugar made from boiling down *tuak*) and beeswax that Father Franz had donated, and by the time we returned to Bali, the new crew members had assembled and the *Sarimanok* (mark two) had been relaunched in the bay. She played gently on the roll of the waves, ignorant of the trials that were coming to her. The staked-out area near her recent winter bed on shore was now the centre of activity. A new temple was being constructed there.

Albrecht was unchanged, still quiet and retiring as he carried out his new duties. He was looking forward to the voyage and did not seem to have any qualms about leaving his Filippino wife and child for so many months.

Robin Davy, a friend of Bob's from Darwin days who had sailed with him on an Indonesian *prahu*, and built a boat with him in the Kangean Islands, had wisely chosen to wait almost until the proposed day of departure to join us. He raked his dark, bushy beard with his finger tips as he told an anecdote, or conducted the words with his stubby hand, with heavier down beats for emphasis, while his relaxed expression advertised his easy-going character like the glow of a fire. He did not allow others to trample him underfoot, however, and his stalwart good nature and common sense were a joy on the voyage.

Colin Putt was the veteran of several Antarctic expeditions, from one of which he had just returned. Though he originated in New Zealand, his frequent reference to his home in the Barossa Valley in Australia showed how much he cared for it. He had been invited over on Bill's instigation since he was so knowledgeable and skilled in expedition and sea matters. Nettie, now back in Bali, claimed that, 'Even I'd feel happy about making the voyage with him on board.'

He made a leather bucket with a wooden rim, while local children looked on and, though he did not speak the language, they seemed to like being around him. He was so patient with their insatiable curiosity and answered happily the never-ending flow of questions from other foreigners. His reputation for telling funny stories preceded him, and he showed his form at evening meals, dominating his part of the table with tales in which his mirth was barely contained, his breathy, suppressed laugh increasing in volume and frequency as the tale neared its end until he had difficulty in delivering the punch line. He was full of spontaneous wit and, having observed the other crew members for a few days and noted their foibles, he replied for me, when I was asked how I preserved the food for the voyage, 'She hides it from Bob.'

The last-minute food preparation was difficult with the increased rain and Don asked an American friend, who dried fruit in ovens commercially in the south of Bali, to send us some. I wanted brown or red rice for its high vitamin and protein content, but I found that Bob, thinking I was doing nothing about it, had asked *Ibu* to get us a hundred kilograms of white rice. It was certainly good stuff, but I was mortified at the implied denunciation of my capability to gather all supplies, and brought some red rice and also some black rice, which is made into a sweet porridge, from the market.

The impeachment of my ability seemed justified, however, when one batch, inspected only in the dark recesses of a storage hut before buying, was found to contain quite a number of weevils. Colin, however, ever ready with a scientific solution, put a cup of bleaching powder and palm vinegar with the infested rice and sealed the lot in a plastic sack. The chlorine produced was expected to kill the beetles, but the acidity of the vinegar was called into question when, on peering hopefully inside after two days, there was no more than a whiff of the gas and the troublesome insects were stomping over the grains as impertinently as before.

Bob was pleased with the drawings and photos of the finer points of *pledang* construction and sailing, though he had now devised his own masthead from what he remembered. Ours included a wooden wishbone with the wings here inserted into the tops of the hollow bamboo legs to hold them apart.

After a fruitless search of nearby Lombok, Don found a supplier of fine, soft palm-weave strips in Bali. I had seen a few lengths of the same material on a market stall, and was told it was used for wrapping dead bodies.

'That sounds unlikely, but rather appropriate,' Bob commented, and got us sewing strips together for sails.

The whole team was working in a frenzy now for the proposed departure date of the first of June. Andrew, an artist friend of Bob's, arrived from Paris to carve the figurehead of the *Sarimanok*.

It had to be a bird, of course, but the large wattles and comb of the creature Andrew created discomfited Bob.

'It's a hen!' he complained, out of the sculptor's hearing. 'He's carved me a fucking farmyard chicken!'

But the fighting cock is venerated in France as a symbol of courage, and when we did reach the shores of lands that had been under the nation's influence, the prow figure commanded much more respect than we felt for it.

Peter Welch was to send us an Argos satellite tracking device so that Bill's estimated fixing of our position could be verified at the end of the voyage by readings made in Toulouse. Navigation was to be only by traditional methods this time, and we would not have access to the information on our position that the Argos was delivering elsewhere. Signals would only be received from us when the satellite was in the correct position every couple of days, so much of the time we would be 'invisible'. The continued reception of bleeps would not give any indication of our condition either. We would have no radio for communication with the rest of the world. Though the Argos could be used to call for help, it would not allow us to say what kind of help we needed, and our first use of the emergency button would end the voyage.

We had drunk our fill of the pageant and splendour of dress and ritual of Balinese Hindu ceremonies, but the blessing of the *Sarimanok* was different. Our boat was the recipient of the holy water, flicked with a flowerhead over the food offerings so gorgeously covering the bow deck. The inedible offerings were consigned to the sea in the time-honoured ceremonial, but the food was consumed as starters before the basins of rice and baked fish were ferried over and the banquet began. *Sarimanok*'s timbers

creaked and groaned under the strain of so many bodies, and the
sailors among us kept an anxious eye out to make sure there
was an even spread of guests on each side deck of the unstable
craft.

Peter arrived with the cameraman on whose acceptance into the
crew our use of the Argos depended, and we all braved the cooling
downpour on the night before the proposed departure to go into
town where a *joget* was being staged. This is an entertainment in
which professional female artistes perform their sensual, sinuous
dances with partners chosen from the audience. On this occasion,
the expedition members and entourage were the major source of
dancers for the *joget*.

We could not leave next day for all was not yet ready, and
it took us two days to cram our supplies aboard. The deck was
choked with baskets of food which could not be stowed as quickly
as Bob, eager to be away, sent them over from the shore. The
night before our departure, a downpour which had threatened
for hours finally turned its fury on us. I had never experienced
such fierce and continuous rain before, and it kept me awake for
much of the night. Poor Colin and Bill had opted to sleep on the
boat to settle in for the voyage and they reported, as they sat
bedraggled in the wind house in the grey dawn, that the roof
of the cabin might as well not be there. They had been soaked in
no time and were physically battered even before the start of the
long voyage.

We were all subdued by the realisation that Bob, who had
read in the almanacs that it does not rain in the Indian Ocean
in June and July, had not thought it necessary to make the roof
waterproof. Since food needed to be re-dried and a solution found,
we felt sure we would not be leaving that day. Bob was determined
to countenance no more hold-ups, however, and under a bright sun
which eventually rose to put new heart in us, we sailed out into the
sea. I was impressed as we left the bay, accompanied by *jukungs*
flying their bright sails and the rubber ducky with the film crew
motoring an erratic path amongst them, that we were only two days
behind schedule.

Headway against the raging current of the Lombok Straits was
only possible with a tow from the ducky and outboard, and we
needed more fuel.

'Anybody got any Indonesian money?' Bob asked as he turned out his pockets so that someone could make a dash for an offshore island.

'No. I thought we'd left the country so I left it behind,' I replied, surprised at my own optimism that we would really get away first time. I had also given up my Ladybird book on sailing for beginners, and the dictionary of sailing terms.

'Too late now if I don't know the basics,' I thought, not expecting to have time to look up vocabulary in a storm. I dusted off my old mastery of a bowline knot and splicing tool, and continued to refer to *batangans*, 'cricket bats' and 'dog's dicks' in the language we all understood.

The money was found, the fuel bought and we 'went to the bottom of Bali and turned right'. Having recovered from the small bout of sickness caused by the violent motion, I turned my attention to the hated kitchen skivvying that seemed to be the only means of securing a berth on this vessel. Unlike Albrecht, who felt he had missed out, I was hoping for a smoother ride than the previous year.

'I hope it vill not be boring zis year,' Albrecht said.

'Oh no! I could do with a bit of "boring",' I replied . . . but his lust for adventure was to prove stronger than my wish for a quiet trip.

Sarimanok on the Indian Ocean

Pride of our galley?

'Would you like to warm up that tea again, darl?' Peter asked.

'Not really,' I replied, rather too honestly.

It was really too much to expect at the end of a hard day. Our newest crew member was Peter Rogers, the cameraman with the dark curly hair and shoulders bent by work, whom we had met only a couple of days before we left. He had been so busy that we did not learn much about him until we were underway, when one of the first facts to emerge was that he loved his tea. He was the only native Australian among us now, and he surprised me the first time he made a request because I thought he was calling me 'doll', but his abbreviation of darling soon won me over.

I had just spent hours getting the fire going and making the tea, and now that it was cold and the difficult fire out, I would not restart it again so late.

'I'd love a cup of coffee!' I thought dreamily. I did not like the Indonesian tea much at any temperature, but coffee would not have been known in South-East Asia by the era we were reliving, and it had to be left off the shopping list.

I suppose the pangs of longing I felt show an addiction to caffeine, and I would have to learn to do without it. Nicotine dependence is stronger, however, and lack of it would prove a harder test for the smokers amongst us. Although the ancestors of the modern Malagasy may have smoked something, such as the modern *kretek* cigarettes made of cloves, they would not have had tobacco, which comes from America. Bob expressed his intention of giving up tobacco for the duration of the voyage for the authenticity of the 'diet', but I thought the sacrifice was too great. He and Albrecht did smoke during the ocean crossing, though they cut down their usual intake substantially. I did not begrudge their 'fix', however, considering the reduced neuroticism in the addicted pair ample reward for the small dent in the 'traditional' nature of the expedition. Since the main Indonesian stimulant of betel nut stains the teeth red, I did not intend to change from smoking to chewing.

'Time for dinner, I hope,' the men muttered among themselves after the long haul out of the straits and an hour or two of shoving things below deck.

Ibu had given us some offerings of flowers and incense to cater for our spiritual needs during the first week, and some cooked rice for our bodily sustenance on the first day. I added some cooked fish I had bought to the wooden plates that Bob had acquired from an antique shop, handed them out, then lit one of the incense sticks on an offering palm tray and placed it in the fire box which I had not yet used. I soon had to face the dreaded reality of life as the cook, however.

There was so little room for firewood in the hold that I had bought *kotoran kelapa* from the coconut oil factory nearby when the Chinese owner pointed out that its energy-producing potential was so much greater than the same volume of other fuels. This black by-product of the edible oil extraction seemed to be the answer to our storage space problem. Along with a sack of copra which Don suggested as a food and fuel back-up, I got in a supply of the black, tarry fuel which we called, unimaginatively, 'black stuff'.

'I can't get this stuff to light,' I whined to whoever would listen when I had held match after burning match to it for ten minutes.

'Let me try,' Peter offered and, using almost the entire contents of a (most untraditional) box of paper tissues, he eventually started a blaze. 'I used to live in Tasmania where it gets cold and we had coal fires,' he said. 'This stuff's like coal – it's hard to light, but when it's going it burns for a long time.'

'We used to have coal fires too,' I recalled. 'I used to freeze for hours trying to get the bloody fire to go. I hope it's not always going to be as hard as this to start it.' But it was.

'Cocktail time!' Bob announced around five-thirty, and on that first evening we began as we meant to go on, though no one over-indulged at sea. Bob brought out the *arak* and mixed some in a bowl with palm sugar and juice from the limes stored under dry sand. I found that like this they kept well for weeks – at least they would have done had we not been so profligate in their use. This period before dinner was a peaceful time. Don proposed a toast to Chico and we hummed a few bars of 'Beyond the Reef', his theme tune.

Sea birds landed on the yard as the sail flew, which was not all that considerate of them, and we were careful about walking below. Frigate birds glided out over the sea, and a white tropic bird with its two long tail feathers could be seen disappearing higher and higher like a maritime skylark.

Bob set up his office in the galley after the cooking was finished, sitting on the floor and writing in the log book at the wooden shelf beside the fire, using light from the beeswax candles Don had made inside pumpkin-like ceramic flowerpots. The candles gutted quickly and could not be used for long, but it was only a matter of days before all such leisurely writing was curtailed by the weather. Early the first night we arranged ourselves in rows on mats on the cabin floor to sleep, and next day the real business of sailing began.

I kept about sixty boxes of matches in different places throughout the boat so that not all would get wet. Matches would not of course have been available over two thousand years ago, but we did not have a hope of making fire by rubbing two dry sticks together, and the idea of keeping a fire going continuously was not feasible with the lack of space for fuel on board. The box of matches in current use nestled in the rice chaff which surrounded the hundred and fifty eggs stored in a large basket. These had been boiled for twenty seconds to form a seal of cooked albumen under the shell, and were coated in coconut oil rather than modern petroleum jelly.

The other crew members had waterproofed the lids of the baskets with melted beeswax, and the large ceramic jars which contained rice and a vast quantity of soya beans were covered with a lid of palm-weave cloth (left over from the sail production) which they also coated with wax. The small mats were fixed on to the jar with a piece of cord tied under the mouth rim. Pork cooked by *Ibu* was sealed in its own fat in one of the good, glazed ceramic pots from the Philippines which had not fallen into a 'black hole' in the village over the winter. This was stoppered with a thick disc of wood whose seal was made airtight by wax painted around the rim.

Bananas that I had dried myself were kept in shallow winnowing baskets hung from the inside of the cabin, as were the dried *tempe* (slabs of fermented soya beans) and my attempts at other dried fruit.

Much of the hull space under the cabin was taken up with large unglazed ceramic jars of drinking water sitting on a kind of deck of their own over the sloshing bilge water. These too were covered with waxed sail material. There was little room left, and most of the dried food was kept out on the bow deck for lack of space below, while the things I needed frequently were stored under the shelf of the tiny galley forward of the bailing space.

The smaller jars of rice which I dipped into every day were kept below the galley deck, which was a couple of feet lower than the outrigger decks. Access to the hold below the galley deck was through a trap-door pulled up from the entrance hole with a cord. The fire was made in a corner by planking it off from the port side of this kitchen so that, when tending the fire in the triangular coral pit, I sailed with my right side or back to our destination.

The storage areas of the boat were in a continuous state of flux. If I needed an item not close enough at hand, I had to rearrange things until it was, and our menu was dictated more than once not only by the necessity of using up perishable items first, but by the facility with which different foods could be reached. It was like a game of solitaire with baskets, played between sessions of removing bones from dried fish and putting them to soak, kindling the fire and preparing spices. When sail changes were made, it was necessary to step over the baskets, or else I would hastily move things out of the way of trampling feet before taking up my position with a rope.

'Time for a bit of exercise before breakfast,' Steve said cheerfully, bracing mind and muscles to the work as he took up the bailing bucket.

To be honest, there was time most days before breakfast to do enough bailing to reclaim the Zuider Zee or build a model of the QE2 from matchsticks (and enough spent matches to do it with), as the fire, once laboriously lit, was not very hot. If the breeze which tumbled down from the sail overhead fed it gently with oxygen, it went well, but the pot on top obstructed the flow, and usually the wind was so strong that it tended to extinguish the fire. I blew on the flames until I was dizzy in an effort to raise the tea water to the boil in sixty minutes, while the rice cooking water took another hour. I had to keep that simmering for over two hours more before the rice was cooked, but the men waited around with superhuman patience, appeased by pieces of coconut sent back as I stabbed my hands trying to cut out pieces to grate.

Chunks came away suddenly and flew through the air. If the fugitive (coconut) flesh only landed on deck, I picked it up and shredded it – and my finger tips – on a grater of rattan thorns, before squeezing out the fatty milk to add to the sweet rice pudding.

'Bloody hell! I wish we still had that *kukuran* from Tawi Tawi!' I complained as the blood flowed from my thumb.

This was a serrated metal disc projecting from a wooden 'horse'. Kneeling on the wooden frame, you could rub the inside of half a coconut over the disc, grating out most of the flesh without the need to prise it free from the shell first. That had been lost over the winter, however, and we had to make do with the rattan torture mac ine.

'Bluddy 'ell!' Don imitated my accent and my favourite imprecation. He did it quite well for an American.

'Let me try,' he said, and took over the monstrous instrument for a while, damaging his hands too.

'You'll get cancer like that,' Bob warned, as I worked over the fire, breathing in the noxious fumes the black stuff produced. 'I don't know why you like the stuff so much.'

I did not like it at all, I now realised, but I had not brought enough wood, which lit much more easily, for the whole journey. The carbon left when the fire was spent was so black that it seemed to drink up the light that fell on it, and it was so fine that it flowed about the probing poker like water. It wafted out of the fire in the smoke and clouds of it blew out of the deep fire-pot placed on top of the coral bed with the smallest puff of wind. I was covered in dust from head to foot, with heavier deposits on my knees and the seat of my shorts, and I looked like a gangling Cinderella, or, on a bad day, the boy who used to crawl up the chimney for the sweep.

The grime also covered everything on the boat, presumably coating our lungs too, as if we were the unfortunate inhabitants of industrial Britain before the clean air act. This was not the kind of

air we expected to breathe out at sea and I was sorry to be the cause
of the unhealthy pollution. The wind soon carried the smoke away
though, and we must have looked, if anyone had been around to
see, like a grubby tramp steamer smudging our way across the
Indian Ocean.

The fire was so difficult to manage that for the first week, at
least, no meal was really satisfactory. The rice was over-cooked
at the bottom of the pot and still crunchy at the top, and Steve's
uninhibited farting testified to its indigestibility. I wrote in a
notebook what we ate at each meal, and day after day I noticed that
the latest was the worst meal I had ever cooked, only to contradict
myself the following day with lamentations over an even worse
effort. When I did finally make a decent meal, it bucked up the
others wonderfully and I was fêted like a cordon bleu chef. When
the feat was repeated several times, spirits rose so high that I was
serenaded with a sentimental rendering of 'Sally, SALLEEE! Pride
of our GALLEY!'

Ibu had given us some *dodol*, sweet sticky cakes of black rice,
palm sugar and coconut milk boiled together for hours and then
cooled. I handed them out with no thought for a possible later
food shortage, just to keep the men happy until their breakfast
came any time between 10am and 1pm. This was foolhardy, but
the supplies of the palm-leaf-wrapped sweets went down so rapidly
that I was not surprised when most crew members admitted to
sneaking them from their hanging basket when *in extremis*, as – I
have to admit – did I.

Confined to the kitchen most of the day doing the boring,
time-consuming and consistently exhausting work of the boat, *was*
a little like being Cinderella, but the Ugly Sisters came around
whenever free to peel the tiny garlic and onions (illegitimate but
welcome intruders in our migrant diet), or grind up cooked beans
in a mortar. Don and Bob also kindled the fire often, but – though
their work was not easy either – one wanted to exchange a day of
watches and helm duty for the responsibility of feeding the crew for
twenty-four hours.

The other work of the boat went on almost unnoticed as I
got up each day at dawn and kept my nose to the grindstone
until dark, sometimes with an hour or two between meals to wash
clothes or bathe.

Colin soon saw where alterations were needed and set about fixing up a handrail of rope from the two front corners of the low cabin to the main mast forestay rope, since without it we had to balance along the gunwale beside the bailing well with no support. His ancient-style leather bucket, though admired for its artistry and ethnicity, was not favoured, however. It was heavy and collapsible, making bailing even more arduous than it usually is, and the non-traditional use of plastic became the norm.

The bailing gap was much more spacious than the previous year's and, on the few occasions I tried my hand at it I found the absence of beams or clutter of any kind on the hull bottom wonderful and the work far less gruelling. The quantity of water coming in this year was much greater, however, and the men worked themselves to exhaustion trying to throw it back as quickly as it came in, often standing thigh-deep in the yellow water.

Peter Rogers, who had nobly agreed to stand watches like everyone else, except Bill and I, in addition to his film work, hated bailing with a vigour that none of the others displayed. Albrecht was not very happy with it either, as he had to stand in the dirty bilge water and expose his leg infections, which were therefore never able to dry properly and heal. Don did his dutifully, and much of Bob's when he was too busy, while Steve attacked the work like a keep-fit fanatic, especially when he was wet and cold. Robin performed the work, like everything, with apparent unconcern, though he certainly disliked it too, and Bob once performed a feverish session during which he virtually mopped up the last drops with a cloth before announcing that everyone else should do it like that in future.

The cabin was much lower than the previous year, though the deck inside was sunk about a foot below the level of that over the outriggers, which meant more space for us and less in the hold. The house was divided into three unequal-sized compartments by the hefty *batangans* spanning the width of the boat, the forward one being further back than on *Sari* mark one. In the small area at the stern, Bill had his bedroom so that he could get up every couple of hours to instruct the helmsman on any necessary changes in the heading.

The large middle part was to be kept free for the rest of us to sleep, as was the small front one. Soft *pandanus* mats were spread

inside the middle section; on the first day the light streamed
in when the wall flaps were tied open on both sides, so that
the inviting interior looked like a Persian boudoir. We lounged
there in off-duty moments for a couple of afternoons and laid
ourselves out like tinned sardines on the mats at night, but this,
like the dry outrigger decks, was a luxury soon to be denied
us.

Waves were higher than in the Sulu and Java Seas and the
splashes which had left the sleeping Smiley unmoved when they
soaked his legs during his frequent naps, now came in more
forcefully every few minutes, even when the hatches had been tied
down. No longer could we lie on the outrigger decks as they rushed
over the surging water. Now the water rose higher and buried the
outriggers a foot deep in the white spume with each swell, keeping
the deck constantly wet and even wooshing between the slats and
up the legs of anyone standing on them, like the spurt of dirty
rainwater which shoots up the leg when treading on a loose city
paving stone.

It was not just the size of the seas, but our angle to them. If
we wanted to reach Madagascar rather than the coast of Tanzania,
or even Arabia, we could not go with the current but had to
resist the northward component of the north-westerly push of
the sea and wind and take the swells on the port quarter (left
back). This confrontation between sea and beat often cascaded
more water from the port side down on the back of the man
bailing than he was ejecting over the eye-level gunwale to starboard.

The shipped water was thrown in so high and so far that it
soaked anyone resting on the cabin roof, splashed through the sides
of the structure wetting the baskets hanging just below the central
ridge inside and giving a rude awakening to the sleepers. During
the day the fire would be dowsed periodically, leaving me in a
hair-tearing rage. Pots of food left out overnight, and the sugar and
water jars tied to the side of the cabin, would be swamped and the
drinking-water jar made from coconut shells would be filled with
salt water where it sat on the galley shelf.

Choppy seas did have advantages, however. After a stormy
night, flying fish could be found on board, some being discovered
dead and past their best in the bilge water a few days later.

'I thought it was my lucky night, last night,' Bill confided on a rare chat with us over 'cocktails', which he did not take at sea 'I felt someone stroking my leg. I thought it was Sally.'

'What!' I cried.

'Wait. I haven't finished.' He silenced me with a raised hand.

' "Stop it Sally!" I said,' he continued, 'but – darn it, – I found it was only a flying fish in my trouser leg.'

We were all woken from time to time by the wet squirming of a fish next to the skin, or found one dead inside the sleeping bag in the morning. The fish tended to fly up in a shoal when moving quickly, perhaps alarmed by a predator, so the morning might bring none at all or as many as fifteen. Once a fish flying right over the cabin struck Robin on the back of the head – more of a tragedy for the fish than for him. They were a delicious change from the chewy, dried version we normally lived on.

After the first two days of fine weather at sea, we were caught in a series of squalls which coalesced into one continuous storm that dogged us for days. There was not a dry place on the boat. All the food in shallow baskets was ruined. The dried bananas smelt alcoholic from their few days' fermentation, but it was not this but their saltiness which relegated them to fish food in the end. All the dried *tempe*, *krepok* (prawn crackers) and the dry ricecakes, like rice crispies, had to go, and *Ibu*'s offerings were too wet for the incense to be lit, so I had to throw them out too.

Much of the fish was wet and had to be lain out on the starboard cabin roof when the sun shone, and brought inside again and covered with a waxed mat when it showered. The yoyo-like action I had to learn was exhausting. I cooked and put things out to dry, watched the sky and got wet bringing the food in again before putting on the waterproofs which I had removed in the heat. When the rain came continuously it was almost preferable because I kept my rubberised suit on all the time and could not even attempt to re-dry the food.

The wind was so strong that we had to bring down the main and put up the mizzen. The sails were laced on to the yard and boom with rope.

'That's not the way the *tukang* told us to do it,' I reminded Bob as he spiralled the rope over the bamboo pole and through the lugs on the sail. 'He said we should bring the rope over the yard, through the lug, then back over the beam on the same side.'

'Oh, yeah. That's right,' he conceded and undid the rope and replaced it as we had learnt.

I was not sure if my interference in sailing matters was appreciated, but Bob did heed my advice occasionally. Throughout the voyage I was called up when sails needed changing and was happy to retain some use in matters other than domestic.

Chaos reigned during sail changes, and after being called out in my unsuitable night gear, I found the mizzen still aloft the next morning. It stayed up most of the time from then on until, just before dawn one morning in a thirty-knot wind, the boom broke the rope lacing and punctured the sail. Peter bravely loosed the sail from the tangle it formed on the mast as it was lowered, but, far from congratulating himself on this, he immediately regretted the action that made him perpetrator of events instead of an observer and recorder.

The steering oars did prove to present too much resistance to the swells, and they were drawn up so that about a metre could be sawn off each blade. The rope securing the end of the oar in case it should break was placed through the newly drilled hole, but the end for securing it to the boat was dropped overboard with the oar, so Don had to go in and retrieve it.

Water was still coming in so inexplicably fast that Bob pulled up pieces of decking to investigate below the water-line. In the bow, he found a neatly drilled hole the size of a ten-pence piece, through which water was gushing as through a breach in a dam.

'Look at that! Wally!' he shouted accusingly at one of our absent entourage who had made such exasperating 'helpers' in Bali. 'He didn't fill in the hole he made to let the rainwater out!'

Bunging the hole up reduced considerably the volume of water taken in, though the waves shipped over the side and the torrential rain still kept the bailers busy.

Colin became ill after only five days at sea. Maybe he should not have come so quickly to the tropics after Antarctica. Perhaps he should not have slept out in that pouring rain the night before we set sail. Anyway he seemed to have something like 'flu, or worse. Don was not well either, and at first I thought I had the sickness too, but it was just the motion of the sea conspiring with the smoke and the unaccustomed *arak*.

Real 'flu (not the heavy cold that many people describe as such) is very debilitating and poor Colin lay on the cabin roof in the rain for about ten days, suffering silently. He could not eat the stodgy, sickly rice I cooked, so I made him scrambled egg instead. Bill, who rarely came away from the stern area, came forward to offer vitamin pills and other things to help. He did it a little sheepishly as if I would disapprove, but here I did think we could make an exception to the 'neolithic' diet.

During the next few days Colin was not the only one who could not eat the sickly black-rice pudding. When I had used up the fresh fruit in banana pancakes and my small reserves of patience on the slow frying taro (potato-like root), we had black rice pudding for breakfast every day and, though Bob still loved it, and Albrecht and Don would eat anything, the rest of us were soon sickened by it. I started making sweet white rice which was better liked, but I found I had lost my sweet tooth for the moment. Bob kindly said, when I told him it made me sick, that I should cook myself an egg instead as a 'cook's perk', but I did not like cheating, and contented myself with a spoonful of the scrambled egg that was all Colin could eat.

One day Bob sat in the galley to confide in me.

'It's serious,' he said. 'Colin just fainted when he went to the loo. He could have fallen overboard.'

He was worried, but watched for another day before making drastic decisions. Colin's unknown illness might prove serious, so Bob decided we should make for Christmas Island or the Cocos which Bill had calculated must be near. Shadow sticks at midday and the stars at night were read skilfully, but the islands were too small for us to be sure of pinpointing them this way and so we retrieved the modern navigating instruments from the sealed trunk. The authorities of Bali had publicly put them in bond to show they would not be used – but this was an emergency.

With sextant, chart and watch, Steve and Bill each fixed our position by dead reckoning. We were already south of Christmas Island which was therefore unattainable, so we made for the Cocos (Keeling) Islands. It was lucky that there was any land in this vast stretch of water, and we were thankful for that, trying to forget our disappointment that we would not now do the whole crossing unbroken. We were unhappy too that we had to throw away the southerly position we had maintained at the expense of such a bumpy, wet ride.

We had been sleeping laid out in a row in the forward part of the cabin, being soaked from shipped waves, and soon decided that it was preferable to sleep on the roof where, though the waves sometimes reached us, the soakings were less frequent or intense. The sea was less chilly than the rain but, though it could be pleasant to stand on an outrigger deck with the water gushing through and warming chilled feet, it was another thing to have a gallon of the stuff in your face in the middle of the night.

My space blanket was snaffled for the helmsman's protection, though there were still the sopping *pandanus* mats to wrap around us as shelter from the screaming wind. On fine nights I enjoyed lying on the roof looking at the stars. I had time to enjoy the romance of our solitude and indulge in flights of fancy, or, secure in at least ten hours' respite from the fire, plan how I would cook something wonderful the next day. One advantage of being cook was that I could rest all night, so long as there were no panics or sail changes.

I was still rebelling against my role as the little woman in the kitchen and could not 'accept things as they are', which Don urged me to do. It's true I could do little else, but I did want at least to feel the tiller in my hand and the wind in the sails sometimes. So far Bob had been adamant that I could do no watches.

'But I did the work well enough last year,' I pleaded.

'It's different now. You wouldn't last half an hour on that tiller. You'd be pleading to get back in the galley,' Bob replied.

Even with the high seas this year making it more tiring, I thought this was a vast exaggeration.

'I wouldn't. Why don't you let me try?' I persisted.

'You couldn't do it. Anyway, you said you wanted to cook.'

I had admitted to wanting to cook if that was the only way I could come on the voyage. The journalist in him must have edited out the last part of the statement.

I was piqued most by what I thought was everyone's concurrence that I was having a relatively easy time. My rage and frustration was like that of a housewife who knows she could do her husband's job as well as he if only she had the opportunity to learn.

Bob was helpful with advice over cooking, and one day started to cook a Spanish omelette with the ingredients I had prepared for making something else. I thought he was doing it for enjoyment and left him to finish it, but found later that this was the second great mistake of my *Sarimanok* career. My foolish letter had damned me as having no spunk, and this incident seemed to show I was lazy too. I was now beyond the pale.

Plastic, though frowned upon from the point of view of authenticity, was our salvation. Peter's film equipment lay out on the roof with a plastic sheet over it. The cameras had nothing to do with our survival, but rice had and, since good waterproof jars such as the migrants probably used could not be obtained, we protected the rice with the modern material too. Dustbin bags surrounded the grains inside many of the permeable jars; when I opened one that had been merely hessian-lined, I found the rice mouldy and smelly at the bottom and sides. We had been too rushed when loading the boat to remove the oven-dried fruit from the plastic bags in which we had transported it. Now they were all the preserved fruit we had left, though some bags were filled with water when the bilge rose up above their shelf in the hold under the galley.

After a week of sailing for the Cocos islands, Colin, who had lain out with gritted teeth in rain and sun for days, seemed to be a little better and I hoped he could continue to Madagascar with us. Bob could not risk another death, however, and the stop would enable us to make some improvements to the vessel.

The cricket bats were doing their work wonderfully, but one on the starboard had come loose from the outrigger, so twisted and tweaked by the sea. Bob shuffled down an S-connector feet first to fix it. From my cabaret floor show seat in the galley I could watch his work whenever I looked up from mine, and I admired the way in which he could bind rattan and tie knots when he was standing on three bamboos (which the planned five had been reduced to) as they plowed through the water. My complaints seemed suddenly so trivial, and I was sorry to keep trying his patience when he had so much more to worry about.

The rain got so bad one morning, I could not even think of trying to light the sopping black stuff, and lay despondently in the comparative dryness inside until it should let up. Bob left me for an hour or two, but when it seemed things would never change, he persuaded me out, and struggled to light the fire for me. Our hands were so wet that the matches were useless before we struck them on the disintegrating box, and when we reached inside our waterproofs for a patch of merely damp clothing to dry a hand on, we scattered rice chaff from the store there.

Mats were draped over the gunwale fence and projected over the fire on strategically placed poles, and eventually we coerced a small flicker of warmth. I warmed up and sweetened leftover rice for breakfast, and peeled taro, the potato-like roots which I liked so much as an alternative to rice, for a dinnertime stew. My fingers were wrinkled at the tips from their long soaking, and I resented the fact that everyone else except the helmsman and Colin, who lay in his green waxed coat like a corpse on the roof, was sitting inside and complaining of the weather. I could hear their laughter and knew I was missing Steve or Bob in good form, dissipating the misery in the best way they knew.

Albrecht was on the helm. Like the rest of us, he had believed the almanacs, but unlike most had not come prepared for the worst. He had only a plastic rain poncho to shelter him from the storms, but carried on his work with a more cheerful expression than I could have mustered. Bob had brought only a waterproof jacket but was happy to accept one of Bill's spare pairs of leggings, boldly labelled with felt-tipped pen as 'Back-Up Number 2'.

Only the previous day Don had called out from the helm, 'What's that orange thing floating by?'

Steve looked quickly up to the mast rungs, then back to the object on the sea.

'Oh no!' he wailed. 'It's my sailing jacket!'

But his lamentation soon took on a comical tone.

'Bye bye!' he shouted back to the waterproof coat, so soon out of reach, and he laughed in a kind of sobbing way, his eyes turned down at the corners, but his mouth bowed up so that he resembled the masks of both comedy and tragedy at once.

He now came out in the unceasing waterfall to do his bailing in the nude since there was no sense in getting his clothes wet. He hurled over bucket after bucket with speed to warm himself, singing and shivering as he did so.

No sooner was the taro stew cooked (sort of) and served out than it was declared to be lunch, a meal I did not have time to cook, and Bob, who had come out again to prepare more spices for the meal, instructed, 'You might as well start cooking the rice for dinner.'

'We've just had dinner,' I flashed back and, having provided two good meals already that monsoon-like day, I refused point blank to struggle any more with the fire. I was saved from too much of a scene by the need for another job to be rapidly completed.

Bob and I had cut the canvas sail-cloth Nettie had insisted on us taking as one of Bill's famous 'back ups' into the appropriate person-sized lengths, almost unable to see each other through the mist of the driving rain from opposite ends of the material. Then all hands not otherwise occupied sat in the gloom of the middle part of the cabin with the hatches tied down and sewed the cloth on to two lengths of bamboo which were to rest on the two *batangans* delimiting the compartment with the cloth slung between. This stretcher would enable the uncomplaining Colin to lie more comfortably, and while he lay silently above us on the roof in the rain, we beavered away on the task as if preparing a surprise party in the room adjacent to the guest of honour.

The sea rolled us from side to side and we were far from the exits at front and back. Without sight of the horizon or the stars, it was easy to imagine we were tipping further than we really were. I felt closed in. We *were* closed in.

If the *Sarimanok* had decided to dip her outrigger low and turn turtle then we would not have been able to climb over the wide *batangans*, across the baskets of food brought into the front compartment, nor go the other way to Bill's area, and out on to the deck before we were submerged. This knowledge was suffocating and our claustrophobia was heightened by the darkness, thickening from the day-long grey to black now that night was falling. As we passed thread and needles from one to the other, stitching by feel or torch light, however, there was a closeness of bodies and kindred spirits as we hurried through the job so that we could return to comparative safety near the front flaps which were not tied down.

I wanted a pee but kept putting it off. I had not taken my waterproof off for days and was sitting in the rain puddle that accumulated inside. When I finally got up, I knelt for a while so that the water would drip off my shorts and collect at the knees, and when I stood it trickled in warm rivulets down my calves on to the water containers below deck.

Mine was the same unisex oilskin of the previous year. It had a long zip down the front for men – no good to me – so, since the streams of rain running down my chin or through the waist seam would soon flush it away, once over the sea on the outrigger deck, I had taken to piddling down the inside of my trouser leg. I found, as Steve declared when he told us unabashed that he did the same, 'It warms your tootsies up lovely!'

This time I began to get out of the suit completely, releasing a warm, rubbery smell from my skin.

'Oh, it's a big job is it?' I was asked. 'They're a pain aren't they?'

As I floundered about in the dark with my waterproofs around my ankles being soaked inside from the sea splashing through, and my sweater now exposed and being drenched by the rain, I could not have agreed more.

That night, we all returned inside, so heavy was the rain. Robin could find only enough space among recumbent bodies to sit for the hour until his shift. We were all peevish by now, and when we spoke of it later, we admitted that by that cold, rainy night we were really at the end of our tether.

As soon as Robin went out into the wind and rain for his watch, I stretched out in the space he had left, callously pleased to be rid of him. I did not stay long though. A large wave roared up and flung itself through the wall, soaking me from head to foot. My blanket was sopping and I sat up and muttered to Don beside me.

'What shall I do? I'm soaked.'

'Will it be better out in the rain?' I chattered on, disturbing his rest.

'Oh, I don't know! Do what you want,' he murmured, closing his eyes to shut me out, and probably wishing he could block his ears too.

I decided to try outside, but the wind was whipping the clothes tied to the mast into a tangle and I was chilled to the bone as soon as I stepped into it. The rain had eased, though, and I tied up the blanket to dry and rolled myself in a mat.

I was so cold, I even considered demanding my space blanket from the helm where it made cold, wet watches more bearable, but to unwrap myself for a while I would lose the little heat I had built up. I fidgeted, shivered and cried, convinced I would die. This was supposed to be the tropics, but I had never been so cold.

'What can I *do? What can* I do?' I hissed into the woven mat.

After an hour I found my blanket was dry! The wind was blowing so strongly that even with the sea splashing up and rain showers coming down it had stripped most of the moisture from the cloth. I hurriedly clasped it around my rain attire, and covered myself again in the mat, heavy with water. My oilskins over wet clothing now acted like a diver's wet suit. Able finally to put less effort into my shivering, I even slept for a while until the bleak dawn.

I had heard mention of a lighthouse looming the night before, but had not dared hope it was true. Now, scanning the horizon from the mast, Steve saw a whale, which did not interest us greatly, and then called, 'Land ahoy!'

Surely not even Madagascar would be so welcome a sight as these small islands were to us now.

Breakfast still needed to be cooked, however, and as excitement mounted and the coast was scanned for a way into the lagoon, I bent, muttering out loud, to the task again. As we neared the edge of the coral atoll, we were wary. The water was shallow and we could easily be wrecked upon the reef as we skirted around the west coast looking for the northern entrance into the lagoon.

A port authority motor launch appeared from the north and Bob negotiated with the Australian captain for a tow. The weather was now lovely with blue skies and brilliant sunshine. When breakfast was over, I lay out on the port deck, quite dry now that the water was calm and no longer spouting up through the slats. The sun slowly banished the chill in my bones, but I was troubled by the smell coming from inside the cabin and the blowflies going in and out through the top slat.

'Looks like the fish's blown, darl,' Peter told me ruefully.

I could not believe it had happened so quickly. We had brought no flies with us, but they had come out to meet us when we were still distant from the land, and the fish, which I had not been able to dry for days, was full of maggots twenty minutes before we set foot on shore.

'Look, here comes the doctor,' Bob pointed out as the Zodiac surfed before a widening wake of foam towards us.

'While they're about it, I wonder if they've got a psychiatrist,' Bob quipped. Perhaps he was not joking. I certainly felt the need of one.

'One of them's a woman!' Steve cried with joy. 'Haven't seen one of those for ages.'

'Hey!' I complained, but I did not count, and the lads were soon in the company of fellow Australians, drinking beer and laughing, and thinking that this enforced stop might not be so bad after all.

Once we had sent Colin off to mainland Australia for treatment (where he recovered without finding out what his illness was) we began to tidy up and repair the boat. I was in a daze and took several days to regain my land-legs on the aptly nicknamed 'Rat Island', where 'yachties' were allowed to camp. We immediately joined in the communal meals and parties and were invited to enjoy their watertight sleeping quarters, modern kitchens and wonderful food.

The island was so beautiful that I could have walked along the white sands and stared out at the azure lagoon for hours, had it not been for the work that needed doing. Our hold stank of decayed copra, which I cleaned out while the Australian children used the *Sarimanok* as a diving board. Our expedition became a study project for the Malay children who, led by their teacher, asked questions with pens poised over notebooks like budding journalists as we dried fish or made new wooden pegs and 'dead eyes' on land.

We dined well during our nineteen-day stay, on fish caught in the lagoon, though Bill, who had openly 'cheated' by eating tinned food for fear of protein deficiency, missed out on this. He had gone to study the weather and seas in a lonely office on West Island, where he had to survive on supermarket food, at two and a half times the price charged to locals.

The booze was cheap, however, and Bob, released from his responsibilities for a while, left us to it. After the first few days, he rarely stayed to work for long before going off to make other arrangements, and to enjoy himself on the other two islands, returning in the evening only to complain at our slow progress.

He cooked in the evenings for all of us, while making it plain to me that he really expected me to be doing this on land too, even though there were now plenty of willing helpers and I was busy preparing for our departure. He actually seemed to be trying to set our new acquaintances against me, and baulked many of my plans for a little well-earned relaxation with them. After an especially vicious dressing-down from him in public, I went with a heart bursting with hatred to continue smoking fish with Robin.

'When we get through all this, we'll be better people for it,' Robin soothed, turning the fish fillets like the cook at a back garden 'barbie', but I could not comfort myself with that. Resentment is damaging, which is why I try to avoid the few people I cannot get on with. I could not do that now.

Don, too, tried to advise me how to deal with Bob's malice in a whispered conversation in the dark sleeping tent.

'He's like a little boy. Don't show it hurts and he'll stop. I learnt a lot from Chico last year. He always used to say "Who cares if you're right?" If your conscience is clear, that's all that matters.'

'I know,' I replied.

'Don't keep saying that!' Don exploded – quietly. 'You always say that, but you still screw up, all the time!'

It was true, but usually I *did* know. It was just putting good sense into practice that was difficult. Everyone, if they are honest with themselves, cares for the good opinion of others, since living among people is so much better if they like you. It required more self-restraint than I possessed to refrain from trying to set a false record straight.

'Just accept things as they are,' said Don, handing me again his touchstones for contentment, and I saw the wisdom of his words, but kept on failing to comply.

'I don't know how I can get through to the end of this trip,' I complained. I was now less worried about being left behind, being on the verge of deserting, prevented only by the regret I would feel when the voyage succeeded without me.

'Just get through each day as it comes,' Don continued. 'We've got through so far. We won't have to put up with him much longer.'

He thought a while longer then commiserated: 'Leaving him to cook that day was a bad move. You've filled Smiley's place now.'

'I know,' I said.   ★ ★ ★

When after two weeks on the island Bill had proclaimed sea conditions satisfactory to set out again, and we still did not move, even Robin grew angry.

'You're captain. You don't seem to want to leave here, but I do. It's about time you pulled your finger out too!'

Frantic activity and boisterous badinage accompanied the last-minute loading. Many of our coconuts had been given away, and I collected the small, sweet ones of the Cocos. A generous 'yachtie' had given Bob a *kukuran* which he, transformed to an exultant adventurer again, presented to me like a birthday gift. The navigation instruments were put in bond again and photographs, which showed no trace of the thoughts passing through the eight heads of the remaining *Sarimanok* crew members, were taken for posterity.

The day was glorious and our friends from the yachts motored out in their tenders to see us off. When the tow boat released us after the passage through the reefs, main and mizzen sails were hauled up and we raced along at five knots. Getting Albrecht, Don and Peter back on board from the tow boat with their photographic equipment intact was tricky. The launch came close to the port quarter and camera bags were swung over to a receiver hugging the stern *pamalong*. Free of their delicate instruments, each photographer in turn jumped into the water and pounded over to the port outrigger.

Peter jumped out too early, and by the time he surfaced, was several yards behind. Blinded by the wake, he did not see the rope we threw him but grabbed it by reflex action when it wriggled close to his hand. He was dragged along behind us for a while, laughing with exhilaration, until we could pull him on deck. I thought he would be half-drowned, but he was glowing with pride at the film he had taken and still not quite sober after the previous night's celebrations.

'What a ride!' he exclaimed. 'We'll soon be there if we keep this speed up!'

'Yeah. Let's go for it!' and we waved goodbye to the launch which turned and motored back to the island, leaving us alone once more.

11. 'Ere we go again!

Soon after retiring, that first night back on the ocean, a commotion on deck drew me out to see an enormous hole in the mainsail. Don and Robin loosened the halyard and rapidly let down the jumping palm-weave, while the rest of us gathered in the rope sheets. As the boom sank to the deck, the yard came within our grasp and was laid beside its fellow among the hastily bunched material, which we tied with cords at intervals along the length of the bamboo supports so that it resembled a sleeve with alternating puffs and gathering, before attention was turned to lacing up another sail for hoisting in its place.

'Grab that rope! No, that one! Come on!' Steve ordered as we struggled to set the sail at the correct angle.

'Is that it?' I asked.

'No! Get the other sheet, fast!' and I swiped at the rope from the yard as it swung by, retaining the one from the boom.

'Pull on that sheet! More!' Steve shouted, the wind snatching his words away.

'Is that right now?'

'Yeah. It'll do,' he replied and we sailed on more slowly until the main could be repaired.

The strength of the wind usually sent *Sari* careering along perilously fast and wore easily through the large sails, which were beginning to rot after their fresh-water soakings from the rain. After a few days, we took to using the storm-sail. This was an ingenious confection of Steve's made from two rectangles of palm-weave supported by some of the network of cord from the Lamalera sail, which was sandwiched between them for strength.

I was apt to get into difficulties when manipulating two ropes, and a moment's loss of vigilance might allow one of them to slide out from the dead eye tied at the edge of the deck. Rethreading it and tying a figure-of-eight in the end to prevent another escape while retaining the other rope, though less problematic by day was incredibly difficult at night. At least I was learning something about sailing, however, and was pleased to be needed outside the kitchen.

I arose at dawn next day and set to the daily struggle again, but breakfast was very late, as usual. Then came the rain.

''Ere we go again,' I thought. 'Nothing's changed,' and went into the food store in the front part of the cabin for a little cry. Don came in and chatted, as if he had not noticed my red eyes, and later showed his contempt for the vagaries of the fire by making sweets from grated coconut and palm sugar fried together in the wok.

There were many flying fish about the decks testifying to the roughness of the sea, but when it rained there were few or none. Perhaps flying fish don't like going out in the rain! A line with a lure and hook was dragged from the helm, though we had no time to fish actively, and Robin pulled in a large tuna which fed us all for two and a half meals.

'Lunch!' I called after boiling the fish head with onions and spices for hours.

'Lunch?!' Steve cried quizzically as he looked up from his sail repairs, and the theatrical mask of comedy spread over his face. 'Hurray!'

I tried sprouting the beans, as I had done successfully on land, sprinkling the beans on a damp cloth, but even when I balanced the large covered wooden plate on top of the rice jars in the store, the seeds were soaked by spray and hardly poked their roots out before giving up the quest for light. The salt was a nuisance in other ways. Clothes never really got dry and, since we had neither time nor patience to towel ourselves down each time we were sprayed with brine, within a few days the crystals left in our hair when the water evaporated felt like dandruff.

On Bill's suggestion, clean drinking water had been brought from the Hyatt Hotel in Bali! The dangers of dirty water registering well with us after Chico's death, I also added purifying tablets to each galley jar refill. The ancient migrants would not have been so protected, but their water was probably not so polluted by dense populations, and they would have built up a resistance to any bugs it might carry from years of usage on land.

The fire, though of wood now, was still uncooperative and the men went around hungry for hours waiting for meals to cook. We were lucky to eat breakfast much before midday and I could not always get the evening meal ready by sundown. After that I would stumble about in the dark washing up saucepans (the men each cleaned their own plate and spoon) and putting beans or black rice to soak for the next morning.

With so much to do, I rarely looked up beyond my domain which did not stretch much beyond my arm's reach. When I did look out to a horizon unbroken by land or ships all around, I was quite overwhelmed by the vastness of this unchanging ocean. I was reminded of the song where the sailors bewail the fact that they joined the navy to see the world: '. . . and what did we see? We saw the sea.' The visible patch of water was as much as I could cope with and I did not really believe there was anything just over the horizon. The world ended at the boundary of my vision. We were at the centre of our universe and were, in a sense, its authors, since ours were the only human eyes witnessing its existence. The arrogance of these thoughts was brought home to me only when I remembered the sea creatures below and the Argos and all the other distant satellite 'eyes' monitoring even this lonely part of the earth's surface.

I tried sleeping inside the first night, hoping the sheets of plastic on the roof would help, but they only stopped rain and, after a soaking in the food store, I slept outside again. I began to get up, thinking I had overslept, when the boat was bathed in light – only to realise that it was bright moonlight that had awoken me. I gazed at the well-lit scene, apparent corpses on the roof, grey sails billowing, and the waves towering up behind the helmsman as the stern sank into a trough between the huge swells. Then, sheltering my eyes thankfully, I slept a while longer.

For rainy nights I sewed together two pieces of plastic sheeting to keep myself dry but, as expected, I was bathed in condensation the next morning and chilled when the insinuating wind evaporated it. It gave me some shelter from the weather, though, and I persevered with my 'bivvy bag' for a few nights, becoming stiff as I put off turning over and disturbing the others with the crackling of the plastic. One night, sleeping with my head to the stern, I moved a little too much and the howling wind caught the bag opening around my neck and billowed it up so that I was like a small piece of meat in an air–filled sausage. I was rustling and fighting to close the bag around me again when Bob called, 'Whoa, do that again, Sal! We increased our speed by two knots just then!'

When Bob sent me into the cabin for the bottle of champagne he'd brought I knew why.

'It's for Chico, isn't it?' I asked.

'Yes. *You* know,' he said, sympathetically.

It was one year since he'd died and Bob made a speech, his voice cracking, sniffing back his tears. I drank first and the froth came down my nose and made me laugh, which did not appear very respectful, though I still thought it better than a public display of sadness. The others took their turn and Don, still mindful of his earthly pleasures, declared, 'Chico should be here to enjoy this,' before he took a swig.

Finally, Steve took the bottle to Albrecht on the helm and the small ceremony was over. There was work to do, but those of us who remembered him thought of Chico even more often.

The front of the starboard outrigger was again suffering the strain of the diagonal thrust of the waves and the downward pull as the boat tipped sideways over each swell. While Bob was tying it to the cricket bat with *cabo negro* rope, a tanker hove into view. It came towards us at speed and for a while we thought we were in danger of being rescued. On getting close, however, the vessel circled us once then reduced its pace to ours and sailed alongside at a hundred yards' distance. It was raining, but the crew were out on the deck braving the dismal weather to look at this strange craft.

'Look! They've got beer,' Steve said, noticing the cans in their hands.

'Oh send us some over,' he wailed, humorously.

'There's a woman there too. Hello!' he waved with renewed vigour.

The crew could see we were not in trouble, but continued alongside for a while. We made large sweeping gestures with the whole arm so that they could see we were pleased by their approach, and they returned the greeting from their metal monster. With no radio we could not communicate more precisely, and, having made substantial changes to their planned timetable already, they hied themselves away over the horizon at great speed.

'Wonder what nationality that was?' we asked each other.

'The name looked German,' I said to Albrecht.

'But I saw the five Olympic rings on the funnel,' replied Bob. 'It must be Greek. What other nationality would spend a fortune in fuel and upset their schedule like that just to come and look?'

(Answer: the Norwegians, as we later discovered.)

Don was now taking regular dips to photograph the boat from unusual angles. Generally he tied himself to the boat and surfed along on the end of a long rope. With the swells breaking over him for much of the time, I was surprised he managed to breathe, but he always popped up again.

He was especially helpful with the fire. Bob sometimes set it up for me and lit it, but usually the occasions when he had the time to do this coincided with the calmer weather and drier wood with which I was adept myself. Don, however, persevered with the damp timber brushing away my thanks with the assertion that he liked a challenge.

'I'm a pyromaniac,' he observed. (A glutton for punishment was the term I would have used.) 'I used to go camping and make fires even when it had been raining for days by getting the sheltered wood from inside the rotten fallen trees. Here, put the pieces of wood you want to burn near the flame to dry them,' he continued as he arranged them around it for me. 'It's hard, but you just don't have to let it beat you.'

He often had the fire lit when I got up in the morning, and might even have the black rice on to boil. He sometimes made 'cookies' and sweets as a kind of recreation on the boat, and with the coconut gratings left after I had squeezed out the oil, he fried up chillies ('Illegal' zest-givers to our diet I was happy to be coerced into bringing from the Cocos) and *terasi*, a paste of slightly fermented fish or shellfish, to liven up the meals. He was just tasting his latest effort one day when an enormous wave came over the side, soaked his head, drowned the spices in the pan, and virtually extinguished the fire. Even Don's enthusiasm was temporarily quelled by that.

The 'black stuff' was abandoned now that we had restocked with woo͏ ͏ ͏ was nowhere on deck it could be kept dry, however, so, when a rice storage jar had been emptied after two or three weeks, I stored a few pieces of kindling in it. The men chopped the wood up for me in the area in front of the galley. It was good of them, since although I could have managed some of this myself, my aim was poor and the main mast forestay was in as great a danger as my fingers and toes.

'Look at that. It's teak,' Robin informed me as he laid into a particularly handsome piece of timber. 'That piece would cost you ten dollars in Australia.'

It was a pity to use such driftwood treasures for the fire, but the store was rifled from time to time, and the sturdiest chunks pulled out for ship repairs.

The food baskets that had sat on the deck forward of the galley now hung inside the cabin where they were less often splashed, but the vacated area did not remain empty for long. Apart from the dehydrating wood, I kept the leftover food there for people to dip into when hungry. I also needed more space than my hole in the ground for preparing food.

'This place is a mess, Sal,' Bob often complained with the implied command to clear it up, but it was not all my doing.

Everyone dumped things there, like coils of rope that they could find no other place for, and if I caught them at it they defended themselves with, 'What else can I do with it?' as they turned their back on the junk which thereby became my responsibility.

As the jumble encroached further in on me, I felt I would scream with the restricted space I had to work in. Whenever sails had to be guided down, the piece of deck had to be cleared in a few seconds for people to walk on and receive the descending sail. The men also came to socialise with me there and, if they chopped, peeled or grated at the same time, it was welcome and therefore bearable, but when they sat right in the galley and swung their legs over the baskets of spices I was using, or rested their feet on the trap-door to the food store below when I needed to open it, they did not seem to understand how aggravating it was, nor did they forgive the quickening of my temper.

On the evening of Bob's birthday, we collected at the bow as we usually did to eat, but this time congregated around the fire to drink Dagmar's champagne, which I had secreted in my bag for six weeks.

'How did you manage to keep that quiet?' Bob asked when I presented it to him.

'That's not all,' I said as I produced a present from behind my back like a performing magician.

The book on Indonesian sailing craft was something I coveted for myself, but had bought for Bob in Bali, seeking signatures on the flyleaf from the helpful Australian Consul, the boat builders and other friends. I felt sure the secrecy had been breached somewhere, but was proud to have secured even Peter Welch's signature, considering the rocky nature of their relations.

'Oh no! It's by Horridge!' Steve exclaimed, when he saw the cover. 'He doesn't think much of him!'

'I forgot,' I said. 'Oh well, with all these names written in he can just think of it as a big birthday card.'

I received an all-forgiving hug from Bob, and a toast to my efforts in the kitchen from Don, but our healths were not drunk in champagne. The knob of the cork broke off, leaving nothing for leverage. The bubbles soon built up inside as the bottle lay ignored on the deck, and we jumped with surprise and dived to save the spuming fluid when the cork popped off, but most of the contents spilled on to the firewood below.

Dagmar had also left her heavy silver chain with me to give to Bob the first time she left, and he wore it ever after until it fell off during a fight with a sail at night. I found it on the strip of deck beside the galley the following morning but it must have slithered between the slats of an outrigger deck the next time the clasp failed, and he was chagrined by its loss.

The turtle rings which Chico, Steve and, this year, Don had given me did not last long either, before breaking or slipping off my finger into the sea, but Chico's gold chain was treasured as a reminder not only of him but of Bob's generosity.

Bob had made a protective flap for firewood on the fore deck, which was effective against rain but not sea, and while on land he had constructed a kind of tepee over the fire to protect it from too strong a down-draught. This too helped, but did not prevent the waves from swamping it periodically. To try to stop them he now built up the port gunwale further with mats supported on a bamboo framework and later added an overhanging roof to the area. He was friendly and talkative during these alterations, and I appreciated his efforts tremendously, but as the fire was progressively protected from heavy draughts, it also forfeited some of the necessary air circulation, and nothing, ultimately, could keep back the force of a shipped wave.

The taro stew I had been simmering all afternoon for the birthday feast would not cook in spite of Bob's inducement with a funnel fashioned from an old winnowing basket. We survived our only night at sea without a second meal by eating *dodol* mixed with my attempt at biscuits made from rice flour, sugar and fat, which would not bind together without an egg. The 'birthday cake' was rather sickly and therefore satisfying in a way.

When, after another three hours' cooking the next morning, the taro stew was finally ready to eat, the boat lurched violently and upset the pot of scalding stew over my foot, though only a little was lost. I had placed the round-bottomed pot in a tightly fitting square basket for stability, and I sometimes shored the pot on the fire with a stick to prevent it tipping, but the movement of the boat was so extreme and unpredictable that it never ceased to surprise us with what it could do. The strange motion of the boat, rolling a little way then stopping abruptly as an outrigger hit the sea, was not only sickening but also made even the smallest task wearying. Albrecht spent precious energy digging out some ointment from his bag when the smoke made my eyes smart.

'Stop Joan-of-Arc-ing it and get a wash,' Bob invited me, after a particularly difficult day spent puffing life into the fire, and offered to take over for a while. I pulled water up from the sea with a bucket on a rope and poured it over my head as I kneeled on the outrigger deck. It was difficult to manoeuvre the soap and keep it within reach, but I lost only one tablet through the deck during the voyage. Clothes were scrubbed on deck and dowsed with sea water, although hair and knickers were sometimes treated to a fresh-water rinse.

The comfortable toilet seat of the S-connectors used the previous year had now been covered by the cricket bat holders, and anyway the water there was turbulent enough to sweep the sitter away, so we usually took our chances ranged along the deck, trusting our lives to the slender shrouds and forestays of the starboard side.

Bob, unlike some of us, had not obtained any warmer clothes on the Cocos and must have shivered under his mat in the point of the bow, where he had moved to escape the wind on the roof. Whenever I watched the waves roll away before the 'chicken' figurehead, it was difficult to guess whether the darkened sodden mats were wrapped around him or not, so well did he cover himself, lying low and still like a log.

We all had sores from the salt water rubbing between our skin and clothes, and whenever we had time lay like beached whales over the peak of the roof with bottoms exposed to the sun. This may have helped healing, but it also made the sores itch. Each person had their own maladies, too. Robin had almost knocked off a thumbnail in the Cocos, Bob had a wrenched shoulder, Steve had piles and Don spots. Bill struck his head quite hard on the roof beams twice when the boat jolted. He went around with a gruesome trickle of blood at the hairline for a day, oblivious of the reason for everyone's horrified expression.

Albrecht's infections were still not healed, but now he suffered from headaches, too. He had become Bill's most frequent assistant with the midday fixes of our position, and this made it necessary for him to stare towards a bright, sometimes glittering, horizon for half an hour a day.

The instrument Bill had devised was a hemisphere built up of progressively larger discs of wood. The largest round was marked with concentric circles labelled with numbers, and in its centre stood a vertical stick. The instrument was so shaped to hang vertically with the board top horizontal, but the motion of the boat swung it too much for this method to be used and, when the sun was at its highest, Albrecht lay on the starboard slope of the cabin roof with his feet on the spare steering oar 'guttering' and the half globe resting on his stomach. With his eye levelled along the flat top of the instrument, he aligned it with the distant junction of sea and sky.

'Now!' he said at the precise moment when all was level, and Bill would read the angle of the sun from the line to which the stick's shadow pointed. From this our position south of the equator could be calculated.

Not knowing the precise time due to the planned absence of an accurate watch, our longitude (position east to west) could not be calculated using the sun's position and had to be estimated from calculations of our speed and the time we had been sailing. This was very difficult, but less crucial than latitude. If we missed Madagascar, we would eventually come to Africa, since the south-easterly wind and swells prevented us from going south of the Cape of Good Hope. It was being pushed too far north that concerned us. Having lost some of our southerly latitude by going to the Cocos, we could now afford even less to allow the forces of nature to carry us along unchallenged.

On Tuesday the sixteenth of July it did not rain. I can state this with confidence because it was such an unusual occurrence that I entered the fact in my diary. Luck was also with us when, about twelve days out of the Cocos, the wind dropped and veered to the north. This allowed us to regain some of our southerly position, though slowly, since our speed was also reduced. Those few days of calm sea were a bonus in other ways, too. The wood remained quite dry and the fire manageable, the sun shone more often and nights were not punctuated by dramatic conflict with the weather. Don undertook his photographic sessions from the water without a safety rope, secure in his ability to catch up with the boat with his powerful front crawl stroke which, like most of what he did, seemed relaxed even when he was in a hurry.

When the boat came to a virtual standstill, Peter took the opportunity to do some underwater filming and we were startled when he popped up beside the starboard just long enough to report, 'There's a whale down here!' before ducking down again to film it.

A small whale had swum up to us and must have found the bottom view of our hull intriguing for it did not hurry on as a pilot whale had some days earlier, but circled around us several times. I dropped what I was doing to swim with him too, but decided I would get a better view from the mast. There we watched the creature spouting at the surface and diving again, its light grey body visible several feet below the water. When he tired of us he finished his game and swam on ahead, while Peter burst to the surface with joy flushing his cheeks and widening his eyes.

'Marvellous,' he uttered as he clambered out.

'My son said he hoped I'd see a whale, but now I can tell him I swam with one!' he said to me, a radiant expression on his face as he dried himself on deck.

The whale was a young one from a school, and for the next few days other graceful, streamlined giants overtook us. I always missed the one that was pointed out since it dived down again and was out of my short sight by the time it rose for another breath, but there were always others following and by the evening of the second day they were like fellow travellers upon whom we rarely troubled to comment.

'Pity we can't harness one of them to drag us south,' Bob remarked, for they were going much faster than we on their migration and, after two days, the schools had passed.

The fire went so well during the calm days that I could leave breakfast cooking for a while, asking the others to add fuel from time to time, and one sunny morning took up Steve's offer of helm duty. The sails were barely billowing with the breeze and the swells were almost stilled, so the heading was more easily judged using Bill's sun compass.

This flat wooden disc was marked out in degrees with times of day marked around the edge. It was placed at the helmsman's feet with the desired heading (205 degrees at that time) pointing at the bow – that is, the direction in which we were aligned.

Bill came out to explain its use.

'The stick goes in here,' he said, placing it into the hole marked by the estimated hour of day around the rim. 'You just steer so that its shadow falls across the centre of the disc and we'll be on a good heading. Make allowance for the passage of time by allowing the shadow to fall further behind the centre, and after about an hour move the stick to the next time-hole.'

I luffed the sails so much in my efforts to go south that Steve joked, 'Freemantle's off now, we've decided to go to Madagascar.'

Having adjusted the tiller, I sat a while longer at the helm, and took advantage of the rare opportunity to enjoy the glint of the sun on the undulating blue water.

The gentle north to north-easterly winds lasted only a few days. One cloudy night we were becalmed and Albrecht and Robin could be heard discussing the ship's light that was moving back and forth in a semi-circle beside us, only to find that it was a low star on the clearer horizon to which our slow yawing had given the illusion of motion.

It was lovely to have the leisure to look up sometimes by day to see flying fish shoot up into our world and stay airborne for what seemed like minutes before flopping down again, or to identify stars with Don or Bob at night. However, I had only just got used to throwing rubbish over the port side so that the wind would not fling it back in my face, when the blast from the south-east reasserted itself, bringing squalls and rough seas. The comparative serenity of the lull was over.

Finding it difficult to perch on the crowded roof without rolling down on to someone else, I returned to sleeping in the food store. Some wind still found its way through the gap at the top of the cabin wall, however, no matter how many pieces of cloth I stuffed into it, and I slept with two sweaters, my waterproof and the buoyancy jacket Colin had left me to keep my back warm.

The rage of the sea was muted inside and I could not believe my ears after a few nights there when I heard an incongruous chirruping sound. There was a cricket in the wood under the deck and even as the wind whistled around us it sang its heart out for mates that were not to be found within hundreds of miles. The poor, lonely creature was a reminder of balmy nights on shore, and his stridulations among the groaning timbers of our flexible boat were consoling.

The dried fish hung over my head in the food store. It banged me on the nose if I lay on my back and there was no position in which I could escape the assault of its smell. Leftover food was now also kept in the store, so I had to take care not to kick the saucepans over in the night. The large jars of rice caused me more concern though. There were three metre-high rice pots lining each wall, retained only near the base by bamboo slats, which were lashed to the *batangans* separating the compartment from the one behind and the bailing trench in front.

These sentinels swayed with the motion of the boat and, as I lay between them, I dared not close my eyes lest they fall and crush my head or chest. I sometimes took up a position with my head to the exit which was flanked by the jars in use, since these were half-empty and therefore not so top-heavy, and only my legs were in danger. The air was fresher near the opening, too, but I could not remain there long since the water and flying fish thrown in were not easy to ignore when they landed on my face. I cordonned the jars to the wall at the first opportunity, only to lose confidence in this when the progressively loosening ropes, which I retied periodically, began to fray.

When the palate was jaded by the daily diet of reconstituted dried fish stew, Bob opened the pork jar. The smell that met us was not as it should be and we found it rancid.

'Sally, listing the food we still had in the Cocos is no good if the food's off,' he complained. 'You should have looked.'

I knew I should have, and kept quiet. The lid cannot have been sealed well enough and water had seeped in. As I tipped out the repugnant meat and cleaned the jar, I noticed a few maggots had found their way in too. Soon after, the deck came alive with blowflies. Then I discovered that the remaining eggs from Bali which had not been discarded in the Cocos were bad. I threw chaff, maggots and eggs overboard, but that did not put an immediate stop to the menace and accusations that came from all sides.

'Where are these flies coming from?' Don asked. 'Why don't you do something, Sally?'

'I have. I've thrown the eggs out, but the larvae must be all over the wood pile now. We'll just have to wait for them all to grow up and come out,' I said.

But the complaints increased with the plague. I turned out the movable things under the deck in the food store and looked for the puparia, but with so many nooks it was impossible to collect them all. Luckily the rest of the food was dry enough not to be attractive to the egg-laying females, and after three days the scourge was past.

Miraculously only one of the rats which ruled the 'yachties', island of the Cocos had walked along the bowline from the palm on shore to which it was secured, and Robin had dealt with the rodent stowaway with a spring trap. Green beetles acquired before the Cocos continued to thrive in the dry fish, and their furry caterpillars carved crevices in the flesh as they ate their way further in. The electric green of the adults could sometimes be seen flying about the boat and we felt like a moving menagerie.

One or two 'blue bottles' – tiny stinging jellyfish – were thrown in with the waves, and a large number of barnacles clung on for a ride.

The green crab that lived on the steering oar was also tenacious. It could be seen balanced on the top of the blade held on by the power of the water rushing over its back, scuttling to a new position only when the top of the blade came out of the water for a moment between dips of the stern. Being on the starboard side, over which rubbish was thrown, it was probably well fed on our scraps and on whatever life had already established itself on the oar, but it eventually disappeared after weeks with us and I can only assume that it made a false move and was swept off, or that it was preyed upon by some creature from the depths.

We were not troubled by other human beings during the voyage and, apart from the Norwegian ship, few other craft were seen. Aeroplanes and a helicopter flew over only once, and we presumed there was an aircraft carrier just over the horizon belonging to one of the several nations with military bases in the ocean. In our creaking ancient craft we were obviously not a threat and not considered worth a second look.

I could not believe how much rice was eaten, and I cooked a little more each day until I reached the optimum amount. Luckily this stopped just short of two saucepans being needed and corresponded to a ceramic cooking pot full to the brim for each meal. After breakfast, I usually cooked the stew all day, then removed it for a while to cook rice nearer to the meal time. I then left this with a 'pot-cosy' of an old pair of jeans or cloth rags wrapped around it in the least draughty part of the food store while I finished cooking the stew.

The dried fish was quite tasty, especially when it had been well soaked to remove much of the salt, and when I cooked it in coconut milk, the strong flavour was mellowed a little. The tuna I had dried myself in Bali was at first filling and savoury, like meat, but when it had sat in storage for weeks and been redried several times, it began to taste like inadequately cured hide. The fish we had dried and smoked in the Cocos was also popular and soon eaten up, but the meagre flesh of the aptly named 'leather jackets' took hours to cut away from the bones and skin.

The red beans were lovely when, after soaking overnight and boiling for several hours, they were fried in lots of spices. They were like roasted peanuts – something we could not bring because the plant originated in South America. They were a rare treat, however, since they took so long to fry that there was little daylight left for cooking the main meal.

Patties of ground cooked beans mixed with spices, and bound together with an egg, were sometimes fried in the coconut oil which went lardy and partly solidified in the cold mornings. They involved a lot of work but were the favourite meal, so there was no shortage of grinders. With the thick *kecap* (sweet soy sauce) they were just like hamburgers.

'Make mine a Big Sal,' Bob called when he saw what was on the menu.

'Okay!' I replied. 'Eat here or take away?'

Black rice, which Bob loved when it was not burnt or overloaded with cinnamon and nutmeg by the ever-experimental Don, soon palled again for most of us. There were rumbles of dissent, especially from Bill and Peter.

'Do you think we could have something else tomorrow, darl?' Peter asked diplomatically, as the spokesman of a deputation. He spoke guardedly as to a savage animal, and seemed to fear I would hit him or jump overboard if he uttered anything resembling criticism (as well I might).

'I'll try,' I promised, but the only alternative was white rice pudding, since frying, which took about four hours, only succeeded in coating the warmed-up rice and onions with oil when the fire was sluggish.

When a couple of kilos of black rice went mouldy in the bottom of a jar, I called Peter over to witness its consignment to the deep, but there was a move back to the dreaded dessert when the drink bought in the Cocos was finished. *Brem* or rice wine can be made from the rice water, and since black rice is sweet, the wine produced from it can be quite potent.

I began to add excess water to the morning rice as it cooked, and after breakfast Robin and Bob could be seen sieving the purple fluid through the edge of a mosquito net and putting it in any containers they could find. The brew seemed to have its own microbes and the water was turned into wine within days, though when yeast was added to help it along, corks popped and bottles exploded with built-up gas. It was not a bad stop-gap, though not particularly potent, and I was assured that the exercise's greatest efficacy was as therapy for the brewers.

There was little time for relaxation for anyone not on watch, since there were sail changes, sewing, wedge making and other repairs to be carried out. The others sometimes managed to read, but I had time only at night when it was difficult as the beeswax candles were almost as reluctant to burn as the fire. I resorted for a while to the cassettes I had brought, with Bill's back-up batteries, but the boat's loud creaking seeped through the headphones and was so alarmingly loud in isolation from other background noises that I kept removing them to find if the boat was really breaking up.

I soon gave up that pastime too. The sounds of the modern world were out of place anyway, and I generally just stared out at the stars or racing clouds to the raucous, but reassuring, sound of the cricket until it was time to sleep. Often when I woke in the night I was entertained by the silhouette of the watch standing on the galley strip of deck to adjust his belt or pull up his trouser legs in preparation for the descent into the bailing well, then lulled to sleep by the rhythmic 'glop' and 'sploosh' of water entering the bucket and cascading over the slats of the deck as it was poured out into the sea.

The cracked front *batangan* bordering the starboard deck had been troubling us for some time. It was still quite a worry but was holding up well after binding and the insertion of a wedge, frequently knocked further under the rattan or replaced by a wider one to tighten it. The condition of the outrigger beyond changed constantly, however, and Don dived spectacularly into the sea to throw a lasso over the upsweeping wooden bird heads at the bow-ends of each piece of bamboo and tie it to the first cricket bat. He tightened this with a Spanish windlass which loosened overnight with the wangling motion, and the next day he crept down to give the wooden baton some more rope-tightening twists before securing it in place. The boat was rushing over the water and Don was borne along on his bamboo 'surfboard' beside us, doing the work in snatches as the poles rose rhythmically over the swells. I turned away to continue my work for a moment and the next time I looked up, he was gone.

Voices were raised at the stern but they were stilled again before I could find the cause. When Don, togged up in thick grey shirt, rain jacket and woolly hat, came to warm himself at the fire, I heard how the force of the water had swept him off the outrigger to the far side from the hull so he could not reach up for one of the S-connectors. When he surfaced and reached out, the boat had nearly passed, so fast were we moving.

'I caught hold of the rattan binding a few inches from the end of the outrigger,' he told me. 'It could have been the end for me, or a coupl'a hours' swim to catch up with the boat after the sails had been dropped.'

'Phew! I was literally holding on with my finger tips,' he continued, and huddled closer to the fire, only to go out an hour later on another photographic dredge through the sea.

Steve tried his best with the outrigger too, and with help tied it to a diagonal splint fixed to the outrigger deck, but this cracked and ·plit at any attempts at binding, so another solution was needed in a hurry.

'I suppose you'll have to cut that broken front bit off sooner or later,' I said, almost to myself, as the posse stood on the deck and mulled over their options.

'Oh you do, do you?' Bob crowed in a who-do-you-think-you-are tone. 'And what's to keep us from turning over then?' he replied scornfully, as if to a half-wit who had not stopped long enough to consider the dangers before blabbing out an opinion.

'Well it's not doing anything now. It's been flapping loose for hours . . .' I ventured further.

After much worry and deliberation, Steve sawed off the offending part, struggling with the blade against the onslaught of the water, while the others prepared to pull the cut piece back on deck with the attached ropes. Surgery complete, they watched for any changes which would indicate the craft had been destabilised, but with the precaution of more weight on the port deck, we continued splendidly, though perhaps with increased drag on that side now that the blunt stump was forcing a turbulent path through the water.

'Ah, she'll be right,' they now agreed.

'Oh well, 'Who cares if you were right?" I thought.

'*I* do,' I had to admit. I knew I could not change Bob now, but I longed so much for the day I would be free of him that I had to stop myself from getting up in the night to slip unseen into the water and swim down, down into the vast depths of the sea.

'Bob says he'll cook tomorrow while you do his watches,' Don told me one evening.

'Wow!' I cried, then became suspicious.

'What's wrong with tomorrow?' I asked.

'Nothing. He just wants to give you a break,' Don replied.

Well, good old Bob. Didn't I always say he had a heart of gold?

Er, no. I didn't actually.

Well, I'm saying it now.

12. She'll be right!

I lowered myself on to the hard deck at the helm around 11pm, snuggled into the extreme tip of the bow and reached for the tiller. Bill had worked out the star and planet paths in detail and I was instructed to steer at 260 degrees – by Saturn, I think. He had made lists of the angle of elevation and times of rising of the heavenly bodies on certain nights for consultation in the wind-sheltered dip in the deck beside his berth, and when Don relieved me at the helm and there was little to be done elsewhere, I sat snug in the hole and studied the information or stared out at the night.

The wind and swells which were so consistent during most of the crossing were an easier indication of our heading, and the only one on cloudy nights. Steering in the stern, I put the hood of my waterproof up to protect my left ear from the wind. There was a cotton thread tell-tale blowing from the mizzen mast backstay, but I liked to look over my left shoulder to watch the bright moon rising and to test that the wind was still right on the port quarter, even though I received a cold blast in the left eye. So this was what the others had been doing here all this time, getting earache and chills in the eye, while the right arm became numb from the gunwale pressing on the blood vessels. What fun I had been missing!

Bob had difficulty lighting the fire and the breakfast he cooked was even later than mine usually was. Robin and Steve brought in the dorado fish which had taunted them by swimming before us like a dolphin for days. There is less preparation and shorter cooking time for fresh fish, and Peter sympathised, 'Pity they caught that today, darl. If you'd been cooking you'd have had an easy day.'

'Never mind. He'll make a better meal out of it than I can,' I replied, and we had *kinilau*, the fish dish we had eaten in the Philippines where the raw flesh is marinaded in vinegar and coconut milk. Bill does not like raw fish and when I called out for more from the helm, where one feels forgotten by the others eating on the foredeck, he passed over much of his meal. It rounded off my day perfectly.

I did my share of the bailing, which was a bonus for Don who had been doing it all on his watch since Bob had injured his shoulder in the Cocos. I enjoyed the healthy fatigue that the sweeping, stretching muscular movements brought compared with the cramped, finicky exertion and twisting about in the confined space of the galley. My lungs were filled to capacity with air cleaner than that which I sucked in to puff at the base of the fire, and at the end of the day, having had some time to relax, I felt I had had a holiday.

Of course, this was due partly to the novelty, but I was pleased to be experiencing the difficulties the others were facing so I could sympathise better, and understand why, after weeks of helm work, Albrecht's tiller arm became painful, then numb and could not be used properly until it had been rested for a few days once we reached land. I realised the difference between being wrenched once from a warmish bed to do a cold, rainy watch and being subjected to the unrelenting routine of three hours on and six hours off, no matter what disturbances or extra duties broke up the rest periods. With so much to do it always impressed me that they could be bothered to shave in their free time.

The next day I cooked again and my knee became swollen, but the day after Bob gave me another break. The red joint was hot, which led me to suppose it was rheumatism. It made kneeling on both knees impossible, so put extra strain on the other, and bending it to climb into the confined space of the food store was painful. I was stitching sails on the roof on my second day 'off' and showed my knee to Bill when he came out at midday.

'Looks like there's fluid in there,' he said. 'Could be all this kneeling you do.'

'Yeah. Perhaps it's housemaid's knee,' I said. 'How appropriate.'

'You're doing great on this trip, Albatross!' Bill said encouragingly.

'Thanks,' I replied, and I felt guilty because though I got through the work, I did not feel I deserved any praise for my constant suppressed anger. I was disappointed in myself.

'Having a woman around brings men up a notch from the neanderthal too,' he said approvingly, and I tried to find excuses for myself in being the only female there, but could come up with no convincing ones.

I did not come begging to return to the galley after a few watches, though on his second day, when faced with the laborious task of making old dried fish edible, it seems Bob might have done the reverse if return to normal duties had not been assured. He was not reduced like me to a feeble jelly by the end of a day of fighting against the motion of the boat to perform every small action in the galley, but he was more sympathetic afterwards.

'Everyone realises you've got the worst job,' he said that evening.

'They do? I wish they'd told me before!' I replied.

'Hang on, Sal. It won't be much longer.'

Robin had been holding this carrot before me since the Cocos Islands and now it seemed it might be true. Bill could rely on his instruments and skill to tell him we were 14 degrees south of the equator and therefore right on line for Diégo-Suarez, the northerly port of Madagascar where we planned to land, situated between 12 and 13 degrees. It was impossible to be more precise about how far west we had travelled and it must have been a constant worry to him that we would miss the tip of the island. We had seen a flock of birds a few days before, but I had already been amazed by how far from land they could go. The water was now greyish rather than blue, however, the pattern of surface movement was different, and there were more fish about which indicated the water was shallower than hitherto. Bill therefore decided he had underestimated our speed slightly. We were closer to Madagascar than he had calculated, since the only shallow water we should cross was the Mascarene Ridge, and he pinpointed a new position on the chart.

'He's even got a back-up position for us now,' Bob scorned.

Bill believed we would take another ten days to reach Madagascar, though Bob set it at six. Having no knowledge with which to hazard a guess, I listened avidly to others' calculations. A kind of lottery was set up where each person tried to guess what day we would land, and I plumped for the ninth of August for no better reason than that nine is my lucky number.

'You can't have the ninth,' Steve said, looking down at me in the galley from his perch on a mast rung. 'That's the day I chose.'

'Well I'm not playing then,' I pouted, pretending to sulk, and secretly hoped it would be sooner still.

Thursday, 1st August

Today I woke to the sound of Bob fishing in the top of a jar for matches and made sure he tied on the lid properly afterwards. Peter helped with the fire while Bob got out the Horridge book and enjoyed picking faults in it. I'm glad that it's appreciated! Don and Robin came along and helped with the fire, then decided to make fritters from soaked dried bananas and batter made from rice flour.

They needed the part of deck in front of the galley to spread out in so I sat in the narrow area in front of that to cut the bones and beetles out of the dried fish, which is now quite disgusting. Bob told me off for littering his sleeping area with smelly fish.

Robin commented on the tiresome slowness of the fire, and the fritters took two hours to make. They were delicious, but Robin left the galley untidy, with flour everywhere and pots to wash. He is not inconsiderate, but did not seem to register the bedlam left behind as he walked along deck distributing his bounty.

Waves were high and as I crouched by the fire, both it and I were soaked – from the starboard side this time, which was quite a novelty!

Friday, 2nd August

We changed to a starboard tack this morning so we are going west-north-west and being splashed from both sides. Don's banana and coconut cookies were salty from the wetting they received. I spent nearly all day simmering small dried fish, and then boiling taro to make 'potato' fishcakes. I fried them all together to make a mash that Steve dubbed 'dog food', though he was the only person who seemed to like it.

Bob complained at the terrible condition of the red beans I had obtained (whose Latin name I am so shamefully ignorant of), which have deteriorated since I bought them from being dried out so many times. Don chided him, though I am less easily provoked these days, and put his grumpiness down to the lack of ciggies now that the supply is nearly spent.

Bill was on the helm for a while and pulled in a huge tuna, so we had steaks for dinner. Lovely!

Peter filmed the men talking about bailing, of which they have done around sixty-four thousand buckets. Albrecht has a theory that you could calculate the distance covered by the number of bucketfuls thrown out.

'At about sixteen to ze mile, ve haf done almost four thousand miles now,' he calculated.

'Have you told Bill about this?' Robin asked.

Saturday, 3rd August

It is four weeks since we left the Cocos Islands and two calendar months since Bali. I hardly slept last night. It was not too wet, but it was windy and I could hear ceramic pots clashing together. I got up and went down into the hatch under the galley to feel out and tie down the empty ones which were rolling about.

I got up very unwillingly just before light with backache again. I think it's the draught that causes it rather than the hardness of the deck. I cooked the rest of the tuna in coconut milk with black pepper as Bob suggested and it was heavenly!

Peter caught another fish, a mackerel, quite early in the day. This shallow water makes a big difference to our catch. We had only caught two others before yesterday. Robin scaled and cleaned it and Bob 'kinilaued' it with the onions I had cut for the stew and, oblivious of the labour over yesterday's now-ignored 'dog food', jollied me along with, '*Another* easy day, Sal!'

We saw some dolphins and stopped work to look. Sunny all day. With Steve fixing the outboard motor in the galley so we'll be ready for anything when we approach land, I had no alternative but to idle in the sun for part of the afternoon. Poor me! While Don finished making his cookies I lounged again, but wearing every scrap of dry clothing I could find now that the cold wind has come up. I'm sorry for those still sleeping up there in this gale.

Sunday, 4th August

It rained a lot last night and Don came into the food store after his bailing to chat and cadge dried bananas. I had one of my periodic anxieties that the boat would turn over and I would not be able to get out through the exit at my feet, so I turned to lie with my head towards the bow for a while. I slept quite well.

Today I found the upturned wok over the embers had succeeded in keeping out dew and spray and the fire was easily rekindled. I spent ages grinding red beans for Big Sals, and Don boiled up black rice, sugar and coconut milk in an attempt to make *dodol*. I managed to clear up after dinner during daylight for a change.

Monday, 5th August

I slept well, but first light came creeping in too early for my liking. We had a good breakfast of bean 'hamburgers', then gybed the storm-sail to return to a port tack. I had too much sun earlier in the day, even though I wore a hat, and felt ill. It seemed to take a long time to get dark after a rainy evening. The approximate time we keep on a clock without a second hand probably needs moving forward again now we are further west.

Bill is worried we will miss Madagascar if we keep to this heading. There is a two-knot current up the east coast which could sweep us past, so we have to try to steer more westerly and it's very uncomfortable and wet.

Tuesday, 6th August

I could not sleep well because of the bumpy movement of the boat. I also found the rope holding up the rice jars frayed right through yesterday, and although I tied the broken ends together again, it doesn't seem secure. The protective hardboard has been taken from the cabin walls to be used elsewhere, so I could not avoid getting splashed even by lying curled up in the centre of the food store.

When I got up, Bob told me the Metzler fell through the deck last night! I went to look, and found that the poles holding the middle part of the port deck have been pulled away from their seating in the gunwale by the constant movement of the outriggers. The weight of the deflated rubber ducky pushed the deck down and it slipped through the gap.

The sea was rough and I looked up at the rat-a-tat-tat of rain which was crisper than usual.

'I don't bu-lieve it!' Bob exclaimed, dropping down on the first syllable of 'believe', all the better to swoop up for emphasis on the second.

He looked up to the source of his incredulity like someone being martyred. There were black clouds overhead and they were pelting us with hail! The small drops of ice fell only for half a minute, but another of our Indian Ocean illusions is now shattered.

The weather was making the sea even rougher and I felt frightened. The swells build up towards Madagascar, and seeing the coast isn't the end of the adventure. We still have the most hazardous task of landing.

In the afternoon I heard a great rush of water and I lunged to remove the pot from the three support stones and save the food. The water thudded against the port side and sluiced over, deluging the fireplace and clattering the extinguished pieces of wood to the galley floor. The fire was obliterated and only a neat hollow in the cold ashes, which seconds before had been glowing embers, remained in the fire box.

The catastrophe was more something to marvel at than to lament, and just when I had relit the fire, land was sighted.

'Where's Diégo-Suarez?' Bob asked and recalled the photocopied profile of the coast Bill handed out to each of us a few days ago.

'There's Windsor Castle,' someone said as they recognised the characteristic fortress shape after which the hill had been named.

'Yeah! We're on it,' Bob agreed happily, and Bill was aggressively ecstatic that his skill had been vindicated.

'Spot-friggin'-on after four thousand motorway miles and no ruddy instruments this side of Jesus Christ!'

'You can throw the pots overboard now, darl! That's what I'd do,' Peter said, trying to draw me into the general celebrations over coconut-shell cups of *brem* and vocal anticipation of dry beds and banquets.

I kept on cooking, however. We were not on land yet and there was no sign of Peter Welch come to spy us out in an aeroplane or boat nor, indeed, of anyone. For all we know, after almost five weeks without contact with the rest of the world's population, it might have been wiped out by a nuclear holocaust. Rough seas viciously pounding the cliffs, discouraging even the neediest fishermen from venturing out, are a more likely explanation, though.

The entrance into Diégo-Suarez harbour is narrow and flanked by reefs. Even modern yachts need help to enter, and with such an unwieldy vessel it would be dangerous to attempt it alone. It's so unlucky we've lost the ducky just now that we need it to go and look for help, though I would not like to motor out in it in these seas. A new support rig has been made for the motor but the swells keep swamping it. When we were as close to the coast as we dared go to search for any vessel that might be coming to meet us, Bob consulted Steve.

'What do you say, Steve? Dare we try it?' he asked, when the final decision had to be made after an hour's speculation.

'No. It's too dangerous. We'll have to go north and round Cap d'Ambre,' he replied dejectedly.

Cursing with frustration at not being able to land after Bill's magnificent feat of navigation, and unable to heave to until morning because of the gale force winds blowing us towards the shore and the tide dragging us northward, we had no choice but to head for the wind shadow of Madagascar.

An enormous mackerel was hooked, soon after our hopes of an end to rice and fish were dashed, but the thin fishing line broke under its weight as it was being hauled up and it was lost. Another disappointment.

Night fell as we raced up the coast to the northernmost tip. The lighthouse there was not lit! Peter tried to illumine the coast we were passing with his filming lamp, but even this powerful spotlight could not shine far enough and as we were pushed on by the gales around the cape, unable to tell how close to the reefs and rocky shore we were being driven, I was sure the long-awaited disaster was at hand. Perhaps many of the ancient migrants were shipwrecked on this rough east coast, renowned for its fierce sharks. We don't want to recreate their voyages as accurately as that!

I sat on the cabin roof and scanned the cliffs, unable even to see where they ended and the sky began. It was not possible to guess how far away they were, and after another hour of this frighteningly blind proximity to the land in high seas and wind, Bob ordered even the small storm sail to be dropped.

I did a little bailing before bed to reduce the load which came above my knees, as in the days of torrential rain and the hole in the hull.

Wednesday, 7th August
Another wet night. When I looked out early the sky was clear

but, standing on tip-toe to scan all around, I could see no sign of land.

'We've drifted away from the coast,' Bob confirmed in a quiet voice which emphasised the anticlimax. 'We'll probably have to go on to Mombassa now.'

'Oh no,' I sighed. 'How long will that take?'

'Ten days, perhaps. It's hard to say.'

I don't think I can stand even one more week in the galley, but at least we have achieved the objective of the expedition, to prove that boats of this kind could have crossed the ocean over two thousand years ago. I congratulated Bob.

'You did it! Even if we don't land there, you've proved your point!'

'Yeah,' he agreed almost absent-mindedly. 'I couldn't have done it without you lot.'

Having given his thanks meekly, he did not waste time savouring his success but returned to his immediate concern.

'We've got enough water to get to Kenya, but that starboard outrigger's falling off,' he pointed out. 'I'll rebind it, but perhaps now we've done what we set out to do, I should call for help.'

In the lee of Madagascar we had time to think and Bill suggested trying to reach the Comores, between Madagascar and Mozambique, since the wind is against us for attempting to reach Nosy Be off the west coast of Madagascar.

After much consideration Bob pulled the alarm button on the Argos satellite tracking device. Then he began composing his excuses to any rescuers who might be perturbed at our using this measure when they find we are not actually sinking.

Robin cut up the yellow-fin tuna that was caught. I am looking forward to good food and an easier cooking day tomorrow.

Thursday, 8th August

With little work to be done, everyone crowded around me in the galley and the restful day I was looking forward to did not materialise. Don told me to 'calm down' and 'take it easy' when the frustration of diving under knees and feet to find things made me whimper. With the general air of vacation around me as I tried to work, these comments only made me feel more bolshie.

We packed our bags since Bob told us the *Sarimanok* could

sink under tow. Robin chopped and ground spices for hours while chatting happily to me, and the fish curry produced was such a masterpiece that when the French navy turned up and insisted that all except Robin, Don and Bob should come on to their ship, I was quite sorry to go and leave it behind.

The grey ship was seen hurtling towards us at about 4.30pm and it was not until we discerned its nationality that we relaxed. They would not be out to capture us for sailing waters we should not be in. I thought I had better get a last shower and threw off all my clothes.

'Look. The moment we sight a ship full of men, Sally does a striptease act for them!' Bob laughed.

It had not occurred to me they would have their binoculars trained upon our craft, but I proceeded anyway, then got my bags together and sat by them as if waiting to be picked up from a railway station.

The large inflatable boat which sped over discharged Eric, the second-in-command of the *Épée*, and took Bob over to the ship standing by, to discuss the situation. He hobbled out of the Zodiac later, the ship's bitch with puppies having bitten him on the foot, to tell us that saving us came free but the tow had to be paid for. He had signed his life away (or rather Peter Welch's) because he did not want to abandon the *Sarimanok*, and two of the crew from the *Épée* were left behind while those of us leaving were ferried over with the baggage.

I managed to show what a land-lubber I am by trapping a painfully swollen knuckle between the wooden steps of the ladder and the ship's side instead of grasping the rope which threads the foot-rests together. When all had safely climbed up from the ducky dancing on the choppy sea, we were herded into the kitchen.

'I'd love a cup of coffee,' I whispered to Bill when I saw the remains of a brew in a jug.

'Shhh!' he said, looking sternly disapproving in case the cook, who was handing out grog, should hear and be offended at my ingratitude.

The hot drink made of rum, lemon and sugar, which is always given to people picked up at sea, was warming and good. As we sipped it we exclaimed, '*C'est bon!*' delightedly to cover our inability to find a subject for conversation with the cook, whose round cheeks glowed with pride and the heat as he relished our enjoyment. (I would not like to work in that large inferno any more than in my tiny, wet galley.)

I feel more as if I'm abroad here than in Asia. The French sailors in their neat navy shorts and sandals seem more foreign than peasants working the land among whom we, in our present scruffy state, would be much less conspicuous. The smell of French cigarettes is lovely, and the language sounds exotic to me now. Even the motion of the ship is different. It rolls predictably from side to side and it is therefore easier to walk on the wide deck than on ours.

We were only seventy miles from Madagascar when we were picked up but must go on to Mayotte a hundred and eight miles away, since the French forces cannot land in Madagascar. Commandant d'Hérouville spoke to us in French in the officers' mess, helped by Eric. Bill was determined to be polite in speaking to the French in their own language, which he speaks quite easily but with a heavy American accent. It was funny to hear him, togged up in his life-jacket with precious log-books scattered about him in a multi-pocketed waistcoat, and with a purse belt bulging with his documents, continuing to speak French to Eric who replied in excellent English.

'*Noo som tray contong de voo vooar,*' he assured the captain.

'Not at all,' Eric replied. 'It is our duty.'

'*Con noos areeverong à Mayotte?*'

'Tomorrhrhow, at night,' we were told.

We fell on their magazines and caught up on all the events which had occupied the world during our effective absence from it, enjoying the softness of upholstery and carpeted floors, though I feared, in my grimy state, that I would contaminate them.

Eating with the captain and second-in-command, we were intimidated by the table-cloth and bowled over by the wine. We began with hors d'oeuvres and bungled the correct use of inaccurately chosen eating utensils. The egg, vegetables and hamburger steak were delicious, but what really pleased me was to eat bread again.

Friday, 9th August

We stretched on the cushioned benches or on the floor for the night but it was stuffy with only two small portholes to the outside and, prickly with excitement, I could not sleep. I had a headache and the unaccustomed motion only made me drowse towards morning when the long-awaited cup of coffee at breakfast woke me to a zombie-like state. Unfortunately, the ship was returning to Mayotte when they were sent to pick us up and was low on supplies. We felt rather guilty at our bread lust when at lunch we discovered we had eaten the last of it for breakfast.

It's lucky the seas were calm or towing would have been impossible. The first harness line broke yesterday as it pulled *Sari* along at seven knots, and when another had been devised, we went slightly slower. From the *Épée* we looked back and waved at the men on the wooden boat, tagging along like a child's wheeled truck on a string. She tipped back like a proud swan breasting the water and at such speed pushed a larger bow wave before her than she could create under sail. She looked so vulnerable, however, that I can hardly believe she has weathered so much. Although I did not enjoy my duties, I have grown to love the boat and felt absurdly jealous of those still aboard. I hope the two French crew there appreciated her – and liked the curry.

Land was sighted as the sun set, pinking the sky behind the hills. The path through the reef at Mayotte was long and tortuous and, the tow rope fouled the propeller, giving the crew the prospect of a hard day's work to free it tomorrow.

Steve's and my 'prediction' of a landing on the ninth unexpectedly came true, and we were given beds at the marine barracks up the road from the harbour. I found my land legs right away after the change of roll on the navy ship, and Bill kept his promise to treat us to dinner in a restaurant in town. As we walked in the dark quiet streets, the hibiscus and frangipani were familiar, and the Ethiopian-like faces of the waiters at the restaurant reminded me of Asia, but everything was brighter and clearer as if the misted and grimed window through which life is usually viewed had been pushed aside. Other senses are more alert, too, and the raw, land world is crowding in through them after weeks of absence.

Bob, Don and Robin arrived looking tired after anchoring out in the harbour. Bob has virtually lost his voice, and his face is even more creased – his eyes more like those of someone woken from too little sleep – than before the voyage. We were partying with the crew of the *Épée*. (The two who had stayed behind on *Sari* did not like the curry, but enjoyed the bailing!) Near midnight the wife of the Indian proprietor asked me, as a sober upright fellow female, to make everyone leave. I gave myself a bad name by urging everyone to go and save the restaurant from being closed by irate authorities, but some wandered into the night to continue the party elsewhere.

Saturday, 10th August

I was roused at various times in the night by the sound of the return from the disco of some of our crew, though I think Bob went back to sleep in *Sari*'s bow. Luckily there is no one else staying in the barracks. I woke in the morning to the sound of singing and marching feet and later found it was the French Foreign Legion, which is stationed here, chorusing like a rough Welsh male voice choir as they do their drill around the port town.

Lying in bed, I found I disagreed with Robert Louis Stevenson on this occasion. It is definitely better to arrive than to travel hopefully, even if it is not the exact destination or method of arrival we had planned. This seems like a lively, friendly place, and it looks as though we could have fun here while we try to get back to Madagascar, if only Bob doesn't change into Mr Hyde again.

Unfortunately he did, though I suffered less now that separation was near. He accused me of 'inviting myself' when we were asked to people's houses, and the offers were sometimes so vague that he may have been right. In private Bob was a little subdued by his backsliding in the Cocos, however, and thanked us for keeping him going when he had run out of steam.

No matter what traits of character I hold against him, he is at least sociable and fully alive. His love of good food and wine made him glory, even more than the rest of us, in the fortune which had brought us to a French colony where the people really know how to enjoy these things. He would not rest and recuperate as I wished to do, and his pursuit of the good life now was something akin to frenzy. Apart from socialising, he had articles to write and did not rest for a moment. He developed a strange giggle which he let out when excited, like bubbles of joy or relief frothing out of him. it was obvious the voyage had taken a great toll and it was some days before he regained his peculiar brand of outward 'normality'.

We learnt that our impeccable timing had ensured our arrival off the coast of Madagascar soon after an alleged attempted coup, which may be the reason for the darkened lighthouse. President Ratsiraka was said to be in Diégo-Suarez to greet us, but the last Argos signal received two days before had led everyone to believe we would arrive on the morning of the seventh. Peter Welch and entourage chased up towards the cape by boat without success, returning seasick and weary to hear that the emergency button on the Argos had been pulled. There was no available Malagasy craft to help, so Peter alerted the French on their protectorate of Mayotte.

We enjoyed the raw African rhythms after the controlled style of Asia. We were entertained to drinks on the *Épée*, and were guests one night at the governor's house, though the hospitality and friendship of legionnaires and civilians alike was just as appreciated. Though the *Sarimanok*, towed by the navy to the shallows, could quite easily be boarded by foot at low tide, people arranged times with us to be shown around her out of politeness.

Something else was keeping the boat private, too, however; the belief that we had come to steal away the body of a Malagasy king washed up long ago on these shores whose grave on a hill nearby had become a shrine. As such we were constantly being watched, we were told, and no one wished to tamper with the possessions of these pale Indonesians.

Bill took an early opportunity to fly away to Europe. Peter Rogers had work in Europe and did not wait for our return to Madagascar either, while Steve returned to Australia soon after Peter Welch arrived to scatter airline tickets among us. Infections were banished and injuries healed by kind doctors who solicitously asked after our health in the street. *Sari*'s wounds were also treated. After she was towed ashore, we fitted her with a short prosthetic bow section to the starboard outrigger. Visitors dropped away one by one and we were left with the problem of a passage to Madagascar. It was no longer necessary to prove a point, but we still wanted to see the country.

Since the wind was against us, Bob arranged a tow to Nosy Be, the tourist-invaded island off the west coast of Madagascar. The motor seized up after only twenty-four hours and there followed days of repairs and drifting into the back of the other boat, until Madagascar came in sight. An onshore wind arose soon after and we raced our former saviours to the land, but we could not enter until after a night spent wallowing at the mouth of the harbour of Hellville.

In the morning a boat came out, just as we were tossing decayed rice and soya beans overboard, and asked, 'Bob Hobman? Where is he?'

'There!' we all said, pointing accusing fingers at the one on whom blame was to be heaped if we were doing anything wrong.

'We will tow you in,' they said after consulting him. And they did.

The welcome was startling. Though we had arrived a month later than expected, the people could still muster a brass band with unrehearsed syncopation and garlands of flowers for our necks. We were wreathed with frangipani, clothed in sarongs and shown to the shade to sit and listen as the governor of the island spoke our praises (I presume) in a language we had never heard before. We were then escorted away in cars and my nightmare of being trapped inside as the boat turned over and sank was dreamt for the last time in the opulent surroundings of the Holiday Inn, where I woke to find the blankets and pillows scattered over the room.

In the following three weeks we dined wonderfully on lobster and avocado and were the centre of attention and admiration. I was touched that the people and government should honour our frivolous achievement, showing the reverence in which they held their own history and ancestors. In the capital, Antananarivo, where the people are more Indonesian in appearance than on the coast, however, I felt uneasy at the lavishness of the welcome, which included a reception at the Hilton, from a poor nation.

It was a strain, too, to play the intrepid adventuress when my self-esteem was at a low ebb, and I resented the lack of freedom involved in being a celebrity. I was burning to see the country and people properly.

Bob had mellowed and was nicer now, but the strain of remaining together with little time for privacy was telling on even the most easy-going crew members, and I hid away in my room whenever we were not actually required by duty to be elsewhere. Our flight to the capital was one day late, and we could not be on time for most of our public engagements because of the five separate souls who were pulling in different directions. The adjective 'sarimanok' even passed into local parlance for a while as something that is expected but never arrives!

I am punctual by nature and felt shamed, as the others probably did, by the reputation we gained as a whole, which might dog us even when we separated. When the men, who had reasons to return to their homes, left the airport amid much hullabaloo, and I stayed on to travel around this country I had waited so long to see, I hoped our acquaintances would grant me a clean sheet on which to write my individual character.

Though I was panting to be alone, when I saw the backs of the other four departing, I felt suddenly lonely. I liked them. Even Bob had good qualities to which I was so often blind, and now I could no longer blame all my inadequacies on him or the boat, nor put off striking out on my own again.

Far from regretting the expedition, I felt privileged that Bob had allowed me to take part. Even so, the prospect of a voyage through Madagascar where I could be free of the chafing of his abrasive personality shone like the light at the end of a long tunnel. The pains of the past year and a half faded as I made new plans.

'Yes,' I thought, as I turned back to the town. 'She'll be right!'

Glossary

Ph = words from Philippine languages
I = words from Indonesian languages ('c' pronounced 'ch')

Ajung (Ph): big boat (i.e. the *Sarimanok* here)
aloha (Hawaiian): love, compassion, mercy, pity; beloved, to love,
  to remember with affection; hello!, farewell!, alas!
arak (I): spirit obtained from distillation of *tuak*
As-salaam 'alaikum (Arabic): 'Peace be with you'; response is *wa
  alaikum as-salaam* = 'and to you be peace'
bahasa (I): language
banka (Ph): small double-outrigger canoe
batangan (Ph): heavy beam right across canoe supporting outrigger
  S-connectors on each side
becak (I): public transport vehicle
bemo (I): *becak* motor
bollo (Ph): machete
brem (I): rice wine made from fermenting rice water
cabo negro (Ph): black, hairy bark of the 'jakka' palm, used for
  making rope
cangkeh (I): clove, grown mostly for the production of *kretek*
  cigarettes
dodol (I): cake of black rice, coconut milk and palm sugar
dukun (I): traditional doctor or healer
es campur (I): 'ice mix'; grated ice with jelly shapes, juice, fruit and
  condensed milk
gabang (Ph): a type of wooden xylophone
gebang (I): palm tree from whose fronds traditional sails are woven
Ibu (I): 'mother'; term of address for mature women

jukung (I): double-outrigger sailing canoe used by Balinese fishermen

kangkong (I, Ph): 'marsh spinach'

katig (Ph): outrigger

kecap (I): ketchup; sweet soy sauce

kretek (I): cigarettes made from cloves

kukuran (I): grater made of serrated metal disc on a stalk, fixed to a wooden board

lapu-lapu (Polinesian?): coral trout, possibly named after the slayer of Captain Cook

ligayen (Ph): a hard wood

Milikan (Ph): 'American'; Western(er); foreign(er)

pamalong (Ph): fore and aft projections of boat like bowsprit and sternpost

pandanus (Latin): genus name of plant from which mats are woven

patok (Ph): adze

pledang (I): large sailing canoe with balancing poles on each side (not outriggers)

sampan (I): (small) canoe

sarimanok (Ph): a Philippine legendary bird which carries a lover to the princess on the moon

sundey (I): small sailing outrigger canoe

tuak (I): palm wine; toddy

tukang (I): skilled workman